I0212172

I Live Alone

我一个人生活

I Live Alone

我一个人生活

Lu Ye

路也

Translated by Ouyang Yu

译者 : 欧阳昱

PUNCHER & WATTMANN

This book is copyright. Apart from any fair dealing for the purposes of study and research, criticism or as otherwise permitted under the Copyright Act, no part may be reproduced by any process without written permission. Inquiries should be made to the publisher.

© Lu Ye 2019

Cover image: Zhao Baokang

First published in 2019

Published by Puncher and Wattmann

PO Box 279

Waratah NSW 2298

Australia

http://www.puncherandwattmann.com

puncherandwattmann@bigpond.com

ISBN 9781925780185

NATIONAL
LIBRARY
OF AUSTRALIA

A catalogue record for this book is available from the National Library of Australia

.

Contents

从今往后

从今往后
守着一盏小灯和一颗心脏
朝向地平线
活下去
从今往后
既不做硬币的正面，也不做它的反面
而是成为另外一枚硬币
从今往后
恺撒的归恺撒，上帝的归上帝
方圆十余里，既无远亲也无近邻
小屋如山谷，回响个人足音
从今往后
东篱下的野菊注定要
活过魏晋
比任何朝代都永恒

From Now On

from now on

I'll keep a tiny lamp and a heart

living, in the direction

of the horizon

from now on

I won't be the obverse or reverse side of a coin

rather, I'll turn into another coin

from now on

what is Caesar's will be Caesar's, and God's, God's

for miles around, there will be no close neighbours or remote relatives

my tiny house like an empty valley, echoing with my own footsteps

and, from now on

the wild chrysanthemums under the eastern fence will be destined

to survive the northern and southern dynasties

more eternal than any one of them

山中信札

我要用这山涧积雪的清冽
作为笔调
写封信给你
寄往整个冬天都未下雪的城里

我决定称呼你"亲爱的"
这三个汉字
像三块烤红薯

我要细数山中岁月
天空的光辉，泥土的深情
沟壑里草树盘根错节成疯人院
晨曦捅破一层窗纸，飞机翅膀拨开暮色
世间万物都安装了马达

我在山中行走
每次走到末路穷途，都想直冲悬崖继续前行
我已经为人生绘制了等高线
我有地图的表情

根据一大片鹅卵石认出旧河床
在崖壁间找到一脉清泉
在田陇参观野兔故居
这些事情，我都急于让你知道

我要细说峭岩上的迎春花怎样悄悄绽放
有一朵如何从它们的辫子
攀援缠绕至我的发梢

我要写到灌木丛里的斑鸠
我真佩服它们
用最简单词语编写歌谣
总把快乐直截了当地叫喊出来

我要讲述太阳
如何下定决心晒我
从表皮晒至内核，把凉了的心尖捂热
把泛潮的小谎言烘干，等待风化
我接受了阳光的再教育

还要提及
每次经过一座躲在阴影里的孤坟

我都担心墓碑上的某个错别字

会妨碍灵魂远行

我要向你汇报

至今还没有遇见老虎

如果万一相遇，我会送它一块松香

跟它讨论一番苏格拉底

还必须说说令人不快之事

最边缘的一片山峦被劈开胸膛，容纳人类的欲望

动物们植物们正打算联名

起诉推土机

我想说，那些气吁喘喘的问题，我都弄明白了

并打定主意

向季节学习抽芽萌长、凋零、萧瑟，向星辰学习闪烁和隐

　　匿

向地球学习公转自转

最重要的是，我要告诉你

经过了这样一个冬天

我依然爱你

在信的结尾

我要用一粒去年的橡树果当句号

落款署名小鼹鼠

我要趁着这山涧积雪尚未融化

快快地把这封信写好

让南风

捎给你

A Letter From the Mountain

I shall write you a letter

in the style of the clean coldness of the piled snow

in this mountain creek

mailing it to the city where no snow falls all winter

I've decided to call you 'My dear' or 'Qin Ai De'

the three Chinese characters

like three baked sweet potatoes

I shall count in detail the months and years in the mountain

the brilliance of the skies and the depths of the earth's emotions

the grasses and trees in the gullies entangled into a madhouse

the first rays of the morning sun that break the window-paper and the

      wings of an airplane that sweep open the twilight

when things of the world are all equipped with a motor

when I walk in the mountain

and come to the end of the road, I have an impulse to keep walking to the

      cliff

and, having drawn the contour lines of a life

I now have features of a map

I recognised the old riverbed from a spread of pebbles

and found a clean spring in the crevice of a cliff face

and I've also visited the residence of wild rabbits amidst the ridges of a
field

I'm eager for you to know all those

I'd like to tell you how the winter jasmine burst into bloom quietly on a
steep rock

and how one of its flowers climbed from their plaits

till it reached the tip of my hair, twining it

I'll write about the turtledoves in the bush

as I really admire them

because they could write their ballads with the simplest of words

shouting out their delight directly

I must talk about the sun

about how it was determined to sun me

from my skin right to my inner core, warming up my cooled heart-tip

and drying up the dampened little lies, waiting for decomposition

as I've received the re-education by the sun

I shall also mention that

whenever I walk past a solitary grave, hidden in the shade

I worry that a mistake made on the grave

might hinder my soul from walking far

I shall report to you that

I still haven't encountered a tiger

and, in the event of meeting one, I shall present him with a piece of resin

discussing Socrates with him

I shall also talk about unpleasant things

such as a hill on the edge being disemboweled for human desire

and how fauna and flora are jointly suing

the bulldozers

I'd like to say that I've worked out those breathless questions

and have made up my mind

that I shall learn how to bud and sprout, to wither and go bleak, from the

      seasons, and how to twinkle and hide, from the stars

and how to revolve around the sun and on its own axis, from the earth

and, most important of all, I shall tell you

that I still love you

after such a winter

I shall end the letter

with last year's acorn, as a full stop

and put my signature to it as a little mole

I shall finish the letter

before the snow melts in the creek

and let the south wind

carry it to you

信号塔

信号塔矗立山巅，孑然一身
相邻的山头上，并无一座母塔与它匹配
独身也是出于对生活的热爱

一个人抵达山巅，还想继续沿钢铁架构攀至塔尖
触一下潮湿的白云，嗅嗅天堂的味道
替人类瞭望一下前程

信号塔不是巴别塔，它只望天而不通天
亦无资格像教堂尖顶那样谈论救赎
它其实类似田纳西那只坛子，让周围荒野朝它聚拢

信号塔上足了发条，令周围空气发痒、微颤
它通知天空一些人间讯息
偶尔也把天上的想法，转发给大地

它采纳风的意见，收集飞行器的心情
它把晴空万里的热度和亮度积攒起来，去抵抗阴霾
它有时截留电缆里的幸福供自己享用

一群蝙蝠穿越信号塔周围的暮色，返回山洞练倒立
这些瞎子自带超声波以遥感未来
只有人类才关心命运，往天上发邮件并渴望得到批示

信号塔仰望天空的力度超过哲学家和圣徒
它每天早晨向天空脱帽致敬
周围山峦全都鞠躬，齐刷刷地配合

信号塔耸立山巅，没给自己留后路
它只拥有一条通往上苍的虚空之路
那条路在时间之外，那条路两旁栽满了小白花

The Signal Tower

the signal tower stands alone on the peak
although there isn't a female one to match it on an adjacent mountain-top
as aloneness is also a love of life

when I, alone, reached the peak, I wanted to continue along the steel frame
    to its top
and touch the wet cloud, smelling the smell of paradise
and watching the future for mankind

no Babel Tower, the signal tower watches the sky, not through the sky
nor is it qualified to talk about redemption like the spire of a church
as it's only similar to the jar in Tennessee, letting the wilderness gather
    around it

the signal tower, all wound up, keeps the surrounding air itchy, shivering
and it keeps the sky informed of humanity
occasionally forwarding the sky's thoughts to the earth

it gathers the wind's opinion as well as the moods of an aircraft
storing the heat and brightness of the cloudless blue skies against the haze
while intercepting the happiness in the cables for its own enjoyment

a group of bats, flying through the dusk around the tower, return to their
      cave to practice the handstand
and these blind things carry supersonic to remotely feel the future
as only human beings are concerned with fate, emailing heavenward, in the
      hope of securing an approval

the power with which the tower looks up towards the sky exceeds
      philosophers and saints
and when it takes off its hat to pay its respects to the sky in the morning
the surrounding hills bow their heads, in complete unison

the tower stands on the peak, leaving no way for its retreat
as it owns only one hollow path to Heaven
a path that lies outside time, lined with small white flowers

盘山路

盘山路充满狂想
高处巨石翻滚，低处页岩层叠

从盘山路远望
相邻两个小山包对峙，在下一盘棋
我的视线随一只鹊鸲移动，我与它共用一颗心

看得见群峰连绵，天蓝，风淡，太阳偏西
一个庄严的大气压
使这个冬日下午光芒万丈

我提着自己的心
越走越远，越走越高，越走越飘，越走越悬
越走越像行在老虎脊背
越走越没退路，感觉与尘世好聚好散

盘山路演示辩证法，我螺旋式上升
这样走下去，需要一根避雷针
需要一顶降落伞，需要在胆量周围
竖起一圈护栏

需要默诵：
"我是困苦忧伤的，
愿救恩将我安置在高处"

盘山路之上，盘山路尽头
天色渐晚，抬头将看到星星伶牙利齿
侧耳会听到天上的说话声

我走在盘山路上，孤身一人像一支部队
这样走下去，一直走下去
会不会在某个拐弯处忽然遇见
迎面走来的我自己？

A Winding Mountain Path

a winding mountain path is filled with wild thoughts
despite the rolling rocks from on high and layers of shale in low places

watching from the winding mountain path
the two small hills stand facing each other, having a game of chess
my line of sight following the movements of a pied harrier, sharing the
    same heart

I can see the continuous peaks, the blue skies, the faint wind and a
    westward sun
a solemn atmosphere
having made this winter afternoon brilliant

holding my own heart
I walk further and higher, the more I walk, the driftier I become and the
    more suspended
as if I were walking on the back of a tiger
with less possibility of a retreat, feeling as though the dusty world is one of
    easy departure

the winding path is demonstrating its dialectics as I spirally ascend
I'll need a lightning rod if I keep walking thus

I'll need a parachute, too, and put a fence around
my guts

I'll need to tell myself in silence:
'but I am poor and sorrowful:
let thy salvation, O God, set me up on high.'

over the winding path and at its end
it's getting dark. If one raises one's head, one will see the sharp-tongued
        stars
and hear voices in the sky

I walk on the path, alone like an army
walking thus, I keep walking
will I perhaps run into myself
at a road bend?

小山坡

下午三点钟，我仰卧在小山坡
阳光在我的上面，我的下面，我的左面，我的右面
我的前面，我的后面
阳光爱我

太阳开始偏西，我仰卧在小山坡
在我的上下左右前后，隔年的衰草柔软又干爽
这片冬末的茅草地如此欢喜
一个慵懒的人

我仰卧在山坡
坡度不大不小，刚好相当于内心的角度
比照某个诗句，把自己当成一只坛子
放在山东，放在一个山坡上

仰卧望天，清风、云朵、蓝天、喜鹊
一道喷气飞机拉出白色雾线
它们按姓氏笔划排列得那么有序
我还望见虚空，望见上帝坐在云端若隐若现

天已过午，人生过半

我独自静静地仰卧在郊外的茅草坡

一个失败者就这样被一座小山托举着

找到了幸福

A Small Hill Slope

at 3pm, I was lying on my back on the small hill slope
the sun above me, below me, on my left, on my right
before me and behind me
the sun loved me

the sun was tilting towards the west as I lay on my back on the small hill
    slope
all around me, down below and up above, the withered grass from last year
    was soft and dry
this land of twitch-grass at the end of winter loved
a lazy person so much

I was lying on my back on the hill slope
it being neither steep nor flat, about the incline of my inner heart
and I regarded myself as a jar, like that in a poem
placed in Shandong, on a slope

lying back and watching the clean wind, the clouds, the blue sky and the
    magpies
as a jet-plane drew a white fog line

in such a neat order that all of them resembled that of the number of
        strokes in a surname
I could also see God sitting on the edge of a cloud, half visible

past the noon now, my life half over
I, alone, lay on the slope of twitch-grass outside the city
a failure, thus held by a small hill
found its own happiness

一个人在火星上

一个人独自居住在火星上
离地球五千万公里
飞船需飞行四年才能到达
一个人居住在火星上
与地球失联，自己跟自己聊天，跳迪斯科
每天遥望地平线和环形山
这些风景，使这里越看越像地球的表亲
一个人居住在火星上
为了求生，通过化学试验来制造水
种植的土豆长势良好
感谢在地球上念过的大学和专业
使自己成为火星上最伟大的植物学家
一个人居住在火星上
这四十五亿年来的第一人
成为这颗红色行星的最高酋长和独裁者
正将整个星球殖民
当想起欧洲、美洲、亚洲，像想起一些村落
感觉当选美国总统也算不了什么
一个人独自居住在火星上
必须启用新的历法

寻找一本火星版《圣经》来读

还会经常想起哥白尼

一个人居住在火星上

饮食起居，一天之中经历前世今生和来世

独自消受以光年计的孤独和幸福

一个人居住在火星上

偶尔设想，假如火星跟金星相撞

作为一个无辜的地球人

那一瞬应该抓住什么当作扶手

最终会被抛甩到哪个轨道

一个人居住在火星

遇到人类发射的太空船遥控车正在工作

会忽发奇想，朝地球扔一块石头，变成陨石

传达星际芳邻的信息

并收藏进航空航天局

一个人居住在火星上，天天胡思乱想

一个人就这样独自居住在火星上

对地球害着怀乡病

想念那边的亲人

期待有人用望远镜看到他

等着有人乘飞船来接他回家

Alone on Mars

one lives alone on Mars

fifty million kilometres from Earth

that a spaceship will take four years to reach

one lives alone on Mars

and, having lost contact with the earth, talks to himself and dances a disco

watching the horizon and the ring mountains

the more he looks at the landscape the more he finds it resembling its

      cousins on Earth

one lives on Mars

and, to live, makes water in a chemical test

feeling thankful for the subjects he has learnt in a university

as the potatoes live well

making himself the greatest botanist on Mars

one lives alone on Mars

the first one in 4.5 billion years

the supreme tribal leader and dictator on this red planet

colonising it right now

when he recalls Europe, the Americas and Asia, like he recalls villages

he gets the feeling that even an American president is nothing

when one lives alone on Mars

one must start using a new calendar

find a Bible of the Mars edition

and recall Copernicus from time to time

one lives alone on Mars

eating and sleeping, experiencing his life, previous, present and future

enjoying his solitude and happiness, calculated in terms of light-years

when one lives alone on Mars

one occasionally wonders if Mars collided with Venus

what handrail he, as an innocent earth-person, would hold onto in that
        instant

and which orbit he would be hurtled into

when one lives on Mars

and bumps into a radio-controlled machine, at work, from a spaceship

one may get it into his head to hurl a stone to Earth, to have it turned into
        a meteorite

carrying the information about its planetary neighbours

and storing it in the Bureau of Aeronautics and Space

when one lives on Mars, one has wild thoughts on a daily basis

one thus lives alone on Mars

feeling nostalgic about the earth

about his loved ones over there

hoping that someone sees him from the telescope

and waiting for a spaceship to take him home

三万英尺之上

在三万英尺之上写信

只能写给上帝

飞机正飞过白令海峡

有些颠簸

上帝以慈祥的目光

目测这架波音787-800

此时给他写信

用汉语、英语还是希伯来语

总之要用巴别塔之后

他变乱了的某种语言来写

这是美国航空公司的航班

中年女空乘的笑容

那么可口可乐

上帝爱我们，也爱这架飞机

我写信是想询问：

亚当和夏娃改过自新之后，可否重返伊甸园？

诺亚的鸽子飞回方舟了吗？

天堂和地狱，两边的人能否彼此望见？

飞机飞到了太阳的藏匿之所

它像一盏灯悬在那里

刺破黑夜，露出青蓝的天

继续飞行两小时，又看到月亮

半张脸亚洲表情，半张脸北美表情

太阳、月亮、地球，宇宙客厅博物架上的

三个小摆设

同时出现在弦窗外

过去、现在和将来排列在一起

与飞机平行

望过去，那么寂寥，竟跟创世纪时

一模一样

Thirty Thousand Feet Above

when I write a letter thirty thousand feet above

I can only write it to God

as the plane is flying across the Bering Strait

slightly vibratory

God is, with His kind eyes

doing a visual inspection of this Boing 787-800

if this was a letter written to Him

would I have to write in Chinese, English or Hebrew?

in any case, I'd have to use some confused language He'd messed with

after the Babel Tower

this is an American Airlines flight

and the middle-aged airhostess smiles

such a coca cola smile

God loves us and also this plane

I'm writing the letter with a question:

when Adam and Eve are rehabilitated, can they return to Eden?

has Noah's dove gone back to the ark?

can people see each other in paradise and Hell?

the plane now has gone into the place where the sun is hiding

like a lamp hanging

piercing the dark night and exposing a blue-green sky

after a continuous flight for two more hours, I see the moon again half its face Asian and the other half, North-American

the sun, the moon, and the earth, like three knick-knacks

appear simultaneously outside the porthole

the past, the present and the future aligned

in parallel with the plane

when I look out the window, they look so solitary, exactly the same

as Genesis

玉米田

大片大片玉米在晴空下做弥撒
在每个州引起回声
这国家拿紫外线当披肩，将玉米田做地毯
这国家的风直吹，不拐弯

天和地离得太近了
玉米的棕色穗子偶尔会擦碰到白色云朵
把彼此的朦胧睡意打断
天是蓝的，田是绿的，蓝绿相交处是地平线

玉米长到地图外、画布外，国境和心境之外
教堂尖顶在颤，那是与上帝保持联络
喷洒农药的飞机多么帅
我站在田边高速路上，能感到地球在转

这里的玉米保持基因中的甜
异于移民旧大陆的命运坎坷的同族弟兄
蟋蟀在它们的脚踝处撒欢
鹰飞过，用翅膀写独立宣言

我这亚洲小型鼹鼠，抱着美洲玉米棒子啃
甜，从原形到比较级再到最高级
没想到可以这样甜
原来我是到了玉米的祖籍、首府和故园

玉米田，玉米田，一个大陆在做扩胸运动
一望无际的玉米田，怎样的肺活量才叫大平原
这个国家心宽体胖
患上一种不治之症叫做：乐观

The Cornfield

vast fields of corn are attending mass under a cloudless sky

creating echoes in every state

for this is a country that uses UV rays as cape shawls and cornfields as

    carpets

its wind blowing straight, without twists and turns

the sky and the earth so close

that the brown corn tassels occasionally touch the white clouds

breaking one another's lingering slumber

the sky blue and the fields green, their intersection the horizon

the corn grown beyond the map, the canvas, the borders of nation and

    heart

the steeple of the church is shivering, in touch with God

and the plane crop-dusting looks so handsome

I, standing in the field by the highway, can feel the turning of the earth

the corn here retains the sweetness of the gene

different from brothers of my own race, migrants of a hard life from an old

    continent

the crickets are enjoying themselves around the ankles of the corn

and as the eagles fly across the place, their wings pen another 'Declaration
    of Independence'
I, a mole from Asia, hug a corncob and bite on it
sweet, sweeter, the sweetest
sweeter than I can imagine
but I am now in the ancestry, the capital and the native home of corn

cornfields, and cornfields, a continent in chest movement
boundless cornfields. To be called Prairie, what lung-power would one
    need?
this country, with a wide heart and fat body
is suffering a condition, called optimism

山坳

秋天正在破产，颜色更加鲜艳
大地的身体里打捞出了一座宫廷
这个在地图上尚未标出的地点，我喜欢。

周围山岗耸立，现在已走到了最凹陷的位置
天是静止的，云是清虚的
溪头那座破旧的亭子应当写进县志
身边的大青石可用来醉眠，这些我都喜欢。

那阳光的恍惚，南飞的绿头鸭的哀愁，石板路的蹉跎和蜿
　　蜒
山那边传来一辆拖拉机突突突突的埋怨
我也喜欢。

如果你唱段京戏，用长腔把我绕进去，让我回到出生以前
让我的身体一咏三叹
我会更加地喜欢。

A Hollow in the Mountain

the autumn is going bankrupt, with even more vivid colours
and a palace is being salvaged from the body of the earth
I, though, like this spot, not identifiable on a map

the mountains standing all around. Now. I've reached the bottom of the
    hollow
the sky still, the clouds clean
the broken pagoda, at the head of the creek, should have been written into
    the county annals
and the big bluestone is where I can lie drunk and asleep—all that I like

the sunlight absent-minded, the green-headed ducks flying south sad, and
    the flagstone street idling and meandering
a tractor on the other side of the mountain is chugging away, complaining
they, too, are what I like

if you sing a number from a Peking Opera, wind me in with your long
    drawn-out tune and take me back to before my birth
setting my soul astir with song
I shall like it all the more

抱着白菜回家

我抱着一棵大白菜

穿着大棉袄，裹着长围巾

疾走在结冰的路面上

在暮色中往家赶

这棵大白菜健康、茁壮、雍容

有北方之美、唐代之美

挨着它，就像挨着了大地的臀部

我抱着一棵大白菜回家

此时厨房里炉火正旺

一块温热的北豆腐

在案板上等着它

我两根胳膊交叉，搂着这棵白菜

感到与它前世有缘

都长在亚洲

都素面朝天

想让它随我的姓氏

想跟她结拜成姊妹

想让天气预报里的白雪提前降临

轻轻覆盖它的前额和头顶

我抱着一棵大白菜

匆匆走过一个又一个高档饭店门口

经过高级轿车，经过穿裘皮大衣和高统靴的女郎

我和我的白菜似在上演一出歌剧

天气越来越冷，心却冒着热气

我抱着一棵大白菜

顶风前行，传递着体温和想法

很像英勇的女游击队员

为破碎的山河

护送着鸡毛信

Going Home Holding a Wonga Bok in My Arms

holding a wonga bok in my arms, I

in a cotton-padded jacket and wrapped with a long shawl

was trotting home on the ice-crusted

road at dusk

the wonga bok was healthy, strong and graceful

with the beauty of the North, the beauty of the Tang Dynasty

hugging it was like hugging the hips of the earth

and I was going home hugging a wonga bok

right now, there was a brisk fire in the kitchen

a piece of warm northern tofu

was waiting for it on the chopping board

my arms folded across my chest, hugging this wonga bok

I felt there was something serendipitous linking it to my previous existence

both grown in Asia

I'd like to name it after me

I'd like her to be my sister

and I'd like to have the forecast snow to cover its forehead and top

by falling before time

I, holding a wonga bok in my arms

hurried past one after another luxurious hotel

one after another luxurious car and woman in fur coat and boots

my wonga bok and I seemed to be staging an opera

our hearts steaming as the weather got colder

I, holding a wonga bok in my arms

braved the wind, conveying my body temperature and my thought

quite like a guerrilla girl

delivering chicken-feather letters

for the broken mountains and rivers

两公里

两公里等于两千米。
不是两千米的跑道
也不是两千米的旅途
是两千米的春光和向往
两千米的汉乐府。
你来的时候，毋须乘舟或骑马
只需安步当车，穿过茂密起来的国槐绿荫。
夕阳给两公里镶上一道金边。
两公里不过是一页铺开来的稿纸
（或者两公里的竹简，两公里的帛）
你就当是从那头写到了这头吧。
空气中有五月沙沙沙的响声
你这个人是最好的汉字，风的手写体
你用穿棕色皮鞋的脚步做语法
让句子辗转在方块砖的地上
每次拐弯都可看作一个自然段落
我的小屋是最忠诚的句号，端坐篇尾
而我，是那小小的落款
正在棉布裙下等你。

Two Kilometres

two kilometres were two thousand metres

not a runway of two thousand metres

nor a journey of two thousand metres

but the spring light and aspiration of two thousand metres

and the Yuefu songs of the Han Dynasty

when you come, take no boats and ride no horses

just walk as if you were taking a carriage,through the thickening leafage of
      the Chinese scholartrees

the setting sun now gilding the edge of the two kilometres

which is but a page of spread manuscript paper

(or bamboo books or even silks)

just imagine that it's written from that end to this end

there is a soughing sound of May in the air

and you, the best Chinese character and handwriting of a wind

create a grammar with your brown-leather-shod steps

letting sentences toss and turn on the brick-cube floor

with each turn that can be regarded as a natural phrase

whereas my hut is the most loyal full s top, sitting upright at the end of the
      article

and I, the tiny signature

waiting for you beneath the cotton-cloth skirt

晚宴

我是黄昏里操劳的女人
挽着袖子，露出细白的臂腕
我从水里捞起嫩生生的菜
刀切在案板上，一下又一下
加重着窗外的暮色
厨房里聚集了对生活的热爱
刚刚燃起的炉火多么温暖

我像只鼹鼠，搬出屯积的食物。
我想在把西红柿和茄子下锅之前
都亲吻上一遍。
烤鸭在印花瓷盘里想着来生。
我找出了颜色焦虑的红糖
准备了一些油盐酱醋，一些葱姜蒜

客人在门厅里。他们和易拉罐一起
等候开饭。
筷子勺子磨拳擦掌
我贤良的笑容是最好的煲汤
在谦卑的屋檐下我找到了幸福

幸福就是包围着我的

热气和油烟

The Dinner

I was a woman hard at work at dusk
my sleeves rolled up, and my fine, white forearms revealed
I scooped up the vegetable from the water
and cut it on the board, again and again
deepening the dusk outside the window
the kitchen gathered my love of life
and the stove fire, just lit, was so warm

like a mole, I moved out the stored food
I'd like to kiss each and every tomato and eggplant
before I put them in the wok
the roast duck was contemplating its next life on the glazed porcelain tray
I found red sugar with an anxious colour
and prepared oil, salt, soy sauce and vinegar, as well as spring onion, ginger
      and garlic

the guests were in the entrance hall, along with pop cans
waiting for the dinner to begin
chopsticks and spoons were ready for a fist fight
my chaste smile the best potted soup
under the modest roof, I found my happiness

and my happiness was the steam and the oily smoke

encircling me

过北极

机舱大屏幕上，银色飞机图标
正移动着经过北极，终于将北极点覆盖住了
地球脑袋上有两个发旋儿
这是北面那一个

可爱的地球，静静地悬着，我从上空飞过
可爱的地球，我喝着咖啡，从弦窗向外俯视
它那磨旧了的自转轴顶端

在北纬90度
方向不是四个而是一个：南方
飞机上的指南针感到多么困惑
所有经线像头发一样收拢到了这里
此处钟点可以是任何地方的时间

北极熊把正在融化的冰面当了翘翘板
鲸从今天游到昨天，又从昨天游回今天
爱斯基摩人在干活，原地转了个身
就已称得上"环球一周"

如果这样抄小路
朝周围看，一切都相隔不远：
中国、俄罗斯、英格兰、美利坚

茫茫白色，白色茫茫，多么形而上学
投在冰面上的暗影，是一架波音747的幻觉
它在万米高空
朝这个巨大磁场致敬

飞机正飞过北极点
我的身体里产生了逆时针的旋涡
心情极昼极夜

飞机飞过北极点
它的盘旋加快了这颗星球的转动
家在地上，人在空中

Crossing the North Pole

on the cabin screen, the silver plane logo
is moving across the North Pole till it finally covers it
there are two hair whorls on the earth
this one being the northern one

the lovely earth, quietly suspended, over which I am flying
the lovely earth, as I'm drinking coffee, looking out through the porthole
at the worn top of its axis of rotation

at 90th degree of northern latitude
there are no four directions, only one: the South
the compass on the plane is puzzled
as all the longitude lines, like hair, are drawn here
where the hour can be the time for everywhere

the polar bears are treating the melting ice like a seesaw
the whales are swimming from today to yesterday and back to today again
the Eskimos, at work, turning around where they are
can be said to have travelled around the world in one go

if one takes a short cut thus
and looks around, nothing is too far:
China, Russia, England and the USA

vast whiteness and white vastness, so metaphysical
the dark shadow over the ice is but the illusion of a Boeing 747
who is paying respect from the height of 10,000 metres
to this huge magnetic field

the plane is flying over the North Pole
as a vortex going against the clock is produced inside my body
my mood moving between extreme day and night

the plane is flying past the North Pole
its circling, quickening the turning of this planet
home on the ground and people, in the air

妇科B超报告单

上面写着——
子宫前位，宫体欠规则，9·1×5·4×4·7cm
后壁有一外突结节1·9×1·8cm，内膜厚0·8cm
附件（左）2·7×1·6cm，（右）2·7×1·8cm
回声清澈均匀

当时我喝水，喝到肚子接近爆炸，两腿酸软
让小腹变薄、变透明，像我穿的乔其纱
这样便于仪器勘探到里面复杂的地形
医生们大约以为在看一只万花筒
一个女人最后的档案，是历史，也是地理

报告单上这些语调客观的叙述性语言
是对一个女人最关健部位的鉴定
像一份学生时代的操行评语
那些数字精确、驯良
暗示每个月都要交出一份聘礼

如果把这份报告转换成描写性语言
就要这样写：它的形状，与其说跟一朵待放的玉兰相仿

不如说更接近一颗水雷

它有纯棉的外罩和绸缎的衬里

它心无城府，潜伏在身体最深处，在一隅或者远郊

偏僻得几乎相当于身体的西域

它以黑暗的隧道、窄小的电梯跟外面和高处相连

它有着虚掩的房门，儿女成群的梦想以及一路衰老下去的

　　勇气

如果换成抒情性语言呢，就该这样写了吧：

啊，这人类的摇篮

生长在一个失败的女人身上

虽有着肥沃的母性，但每次都到一个胚芽为止

啊，这爱情的教堂

它是N次恋爱的废墟，仿佛圆明园

这另一颗心脏，全身最孤独最空旷的器官

啊，它本是房屋一幢故园一座，却时常感到无家可归

它不相信地心引力，它有柔软潮润的直觉

有飞的记忆

B-Mode Ultrasound Report, Gynecology Department

on it is written:

anteversion of uterus and abnormal corpus uteri: 9.1 x 5.4 x 4.7cm

a prominent tubercle on the back wall that is 1.9 x 1.8cm

its inner membrane 0.8cm in thickness

the appendix (on the left) is 2.7 x 1.6cm and (on the right) 2.7 x 1.8cm

with a clear and even echo

I was drinking till my belly was close to bursting, my legs weakening

and my lower abdomen turned thin and transparent, like the crepe

    georgette I was in

to make it easier for the instrument to explore the complex topography

    inside

the doctors thought they were looking at a kaleidoscope

a woman's final file, her history as much as her geography

the descriptive language on the report, in an objective tone

is an assessment of the most vital part of a woman

like the remarks on a student's performance at school in the old days

the figures accurate and submissive

suggesting that one had to offer a monthly betrothal present

if the report were written in a figurative language

it would have to be something like this: its shape is closer to a torpedo than an opening magnolia denudata

with a garment of pure cotton and silk linings

hiding nothing in her heart except the depths of her body, in a corner or a
    far suburb

so remote it almost resembles the western regions in the body

connected to the outside and heights by dark channels and narrow lifts

with a door ajar, a dream of crowded kids and the courage to be ageing all
    the way

in a lyrical language, it would have to be written thus:

ah, this cradle of mankind

grown on the body of a failed woman

stops short of germinating despite its rich maternal instinct

ah, this church of love

ruins of love to the nth degree, like the Imperial Summer Palace

this other heart, an organ the most solitary and empty in the body

ah, instead of being a house, an old garden, it often feels homeless

and does not believe in gravitation as it has an intuition, soft and moist

a memory that flies

一床棉被

妈妈在窗下给我缝被子
用操劳的针穿起了牵挂的线。
我歪坐床头，脚丫子放上书桌
我是她的女儿。

十年前，姥爷到集上买布料和棉花
请姨姥姥做了这床被子。
姨姥姥是妈妈的亲姨，姥姥的亲妹妹
穿针引线时想起她那早逝的姐姐。
姥爷在一个有薄雾的清晨抱着新被子
比冬天早一步赶到城里。
那时我在恋爱，对自家人态度漠然。

姥爷于前年年底去世
他对我的挂念以一床棉被的形式
留在了人间。
棉花是上好的，洁白、善良、厚道
那是一床棉被的传统美德
布料图案上的野菊盛开
如今陷在怀念里，枝叶花瓣看上去有点疼。

我把脸贴在棉被上。

我挨着死去的和正在衰老的亲人

挨着二十四节气和大地体温

上面有姥姥味、姥爷味、姨姥姥味和妈妈味

母系家族的爱多么绵软多么悠长

我是大家最惦记的那个孩子

A Cotton Quilt

Mom is sewing the quilt for me by the window
her busy needle picking up a concerned thread
I sit across the bed, my feet on the desk
I, her daughter

10 years ago, when Grandpa went to the market to buy cloth and cotton
he asked Grand Aunty to sew up this quilt
Aunty is Mom's blood aunty, Grandma's younger sister
when she sewed it she thought of her long dead sister
on a misty early morning, Grandpa was holding this new quilt
hurried into the city, one step earlier than the winter
I was in love at the time, and was quite cold towards family

Grandpa died at the end of last year
his affection for me, though, lingers
in the form of a quilt
the cotton is of supreme quality, pure-white, good and honest
a quilt of traditional virtues
the cloth pattern with wild chrysanthemum in bloom
its branches and petals, now caught in the yearning, look painful

I hold my face against the quilt

I am with my loved ones, dead or ageing

and I am with the twenty-four solar terms and the bodily temperature of
the earth

it sends forth a smell mixed with Grandma, Grandpa, Grand Aunty and
Mom

the love of the matriarchal family softens and lingers

and I am the child they have all cared so much about

也许我愿意

也许我愿意
每天和你在一起
放鸭子。
我后半生的心
是一块擦拭得锃亮的
窗玻璃。
我们一大早就去了不远处
那条心地单纯的小溪
太阳在皮肤上涂上一层
深色的釉彩
健康的青草漫过双膝。
我愿意
每天黄昏听你
用口哨集合起鸭子回家
那时大地多么沉寂
落日多么辉煌、壮丽。
由于水草丰茂
我们的鸭子长得太大，几乎像鹅
只是头顶上缺少红色王冠
那才是鹅的标志。

我们不擅管理

使得鸭子们全都跟我们一样

信奉生活中的诗意

渐渐夜不归宿，踏上伟大的流浪之路

哪管快乐和失意

就这样，它们从人工养殖过渡还原成了

野鸭子

把自由主义的蛋，一颗一颗地

产在无边的草丛里。

Perhaps I Am Willing

perhaps I am willing

to be with you every day

raising ducks.

my heart, for the rest of my life

is a window pane

cleaned till it shines.

early in the morning we go somewhere near

to the simple-minded creek

the sun spreading our skins

with a deep glaze

and the healthy grass reaching over our knees.

I am willing

to listen to you every dusk

gathering the ducks home with a whistle

when the land becomes quiet

and the sun, brilliant, beautiful.

because of the lush water grass

our ducks are over-grown, nearly to the size of geese

without the red crown

the sign of the geese.

we are so poor at managing them

that these ducks have become like us

believing only in the poetry of life

not wanting to go home for the night, and stepping onto a great wandering

      journey

happy or unhappy

until they move back, from artificial propagation

to wilderness

laying liberalist eggs, one by one

in the boundless grass.

你在病中

我隔了上千里烟雨迷蒙的国土
惦念着你的病情
竟把天气预报误读成心电图、CT、彩超和血压数
我还要为此斋戒，只吃一点少油的素菜米粥
祈祷你的康复

如今你在病中
请像一棵雨后的稗草那样好好歇息
在午后阳光下闪烁细细的嫩芽
把来苏水味的疼痛和晕眩打电话告诉我吧
生命原是一笔需要慢慢偿还的债务
请打开病房的窗户，看看水杉树顶的朝霞和落日
还有那飘着晚饭花香气的小路
安宁和静默是最好的大夫

我还有一大串叮嘱，也请求你一一记住：
你要在美德里加进去那么一点儿懒
让书桌上轻轻落着尘土
你要与茶为友，以烟酒为敌
你要常吃核桃花生芝麻，还有海藻和鱼

你要每天去江边散散步

你必须按时吃药啊，不能怕苦

You Have Fallen Ill

separated from you by hundreds of kilometres of a rainy land

I am so concerned about your condition

I misread weather report as cardiograph, CT, colour ultrasound or blood

pressure figures

I shall fast for you, taking only vegetables with little oil and rice congee

and pray for your recovery

now that you are ill

please take a good rest like barn grass after the rain

flashing your tender bud in the afternoon sun

ring me about your pain and dizziness smelling of Lysol

for life is a debt that needs to be paid off slowly

please open the ward window and see the morning glow and the setting

     sun over the top of the dawn redwood

and the path drifting with the aroma of dinner flower

peace and quiet are the best doctors

I have so many things to warn you about but please do remember these:

you have to add a bit of laziness to your virtue

and let the dust gently settle on your desk

make friends with tea and enemies with liquor or cigarettes

have walnuts, peanuts, sesame, seaweeds and fish

take a regular walk along the river

and take medications on time, not afraid of their bitterness

单数

如今，一切由双数变成了单数
棉被一床，枕头一个
牙刷一只，毛巾一条
椅子一把，照片保留单人的
窗外杨树也只有一棵
还有，每月照例徒劳地排出卵子一个
所有这些事物都是雌的
她们像寡妇一样形影相吊
像尼姑一样固守贞操

如今，一个人锁门，一个人下楼
一个人逛商店，一个人散步，一个人回屋
一个人看书，一个人大摆宴席，一个人睡去
一个人从早晨过到晚上
还要一个人走向生命的尽头
布娃娃在书架上落满灰尘
跟我一样也没有配偶
我离异了，而她是老姑娘
我们同病却无法相怜

电话机聋哑人似地不声不响

谁能在夜深人静时拨通我的心弦

我连心跳的每一下都是孤零零的

在空荡荡的房子里引起回音

我是韵母找不到声母

我是仄声找不到平声

我是火柴皮找不到火柴棒

我是抛物线找不到坐标系

我是蒲公英找不到春天找不到风

我是单数，我是"1"

以孤单为使命

以寂寞为事业

One

now, everything has turned from two into one
one cotton quilt, one pillow
one tooth-brush, one face-towel
one chair, and photographs that contain only one person
and there is only one poplar tree outside the window as well
what's more, I emit one egg in vain as usual every month
all these things are feminine
shadows matching their shapes, like a widow
sticking to her chastity, like a nun

now, I lock my door alone, I walk downstairs alone
I window-shop alone, I walk alone, I go back to my room alone
I read alone, I have a banquet alone, I sleep alone
I live from morning till night
and have to walk to the end of my life alone
the cloth doll, covered in dust, on the bookshelf
has no spouse, like myself
I am a divorcee and she, an old maid
we suffer from the same condition but have no pity for one another

my telephone remains silent, like a mute
who can strike my heart's cord in the stillness of the night?

even my heartbeat is solitary

creating an echo in the empty room

I am a compound vowel that cannot find a matching consonant

I am an oblique tone that cannot find a matching level tone

I am a surface that cannot find a match to strike

I am a parabola that cannot find its coordinate system

and I am a dandelion that can find neither the spring nor the wind

I am one, and I am '1'

with solitude as my mission

and loneliness as my career

国际航班

跨出汉语的城墙
穿过日语的断臂残垣，翻过韩文的篱笆
最后，又跳进了英语的圆窗
我被译来译去，成了一个病句

激情每小时上千公里
窗外是太阳的打谷场和白云的村庄
我相信是一场三万英尺的大风把我刮走
将荒唐的前半生扔在了地球上

国际日期变更线像一条跳绳
我从4月12日跳回11日
今天变昨天，错是否能改，爱是否可以重来

The International Flight

across the city wall of the Chinese language
through the broken limbs of the Japanese language and over the hedge of
    the Korean language
until I, with a leap into the round window of the English language
am translated into a sick sentence

passion covers more than a thousand kilometres an hour
there are the sun-threshing-ground and cloud-villages outside the window
it is a gale, I believe, of thirty-thousand feet that is blowing me away
chucking the absurd first part of my life onto the earth

the International Date Line resembles a jumping rope
as I jump back from the 12th to the 11th
from today to yesterday: Can mistakes be corrected? Can love return?

大雪

睡眠昏沉：从凌晨到晌午，直至黄昏
把星期四睡成了礼拜天
当醒来，看到窗外白雪皑皑
我想，一定是我的昏睡招致了这场茫茫大雪

我还想，如果我睡的时间短些，引起的会是小雪或雨加雪
如果浅睡，招致的将是一场绵绵细雨
如果我只是小睡或打个盹呢，天就只是阴下来
要是我压根没睡，当然了，天还会是晴的

这场大雪一定与我长时间的昏睡有关
安眠使得所有郁闷都化为水汽又结成了冰晶
我身体里的冬天履带辚辚，辗过西伯利亚，翻越珠穆朗玛
在一个梦的边境停下

Big Snow

heady sleep: from early morning to noon till dusk
turning Thursday into a Sunday
when I woke up and saw whiteness outside the window
I thought that my dizzy sleep must have induced this huge snow

I was also thinking to myself: if I had slept less it might have been a
        smaller snow or a sleet
if it were a shallow sleep, it might have been a drizzle
or if I had only taken a nap or dozed away, it might have been overcast
and if I didn't fall asleep, it would certainly have been fine

the snow must have somehow related to my long sleep
the peaceful slumber evaporating all my melancholy then freezing it
the winter, inside my body, was running on its rumbling tracks, through
        Siberia and over the Himalayas
stopping at the edge of a dream

女生宿舍

其实女生宿舍就相当于
古代小姐的闺房
如果念的是中文系
那就算是潇湘馆或蘅芜苑了

窗外晾晒的衣裙正值妙龄
被阳光哄骗又滋养
楼下槐树影里总有男生贮立
失魂落魄，个个像贾宝玉或张君瑞
挂风铃的窗口在虔诚的目光里
被仰望成革命圣地的宝塔
这是通往爱情的最后一站，如同
前哨阵地

像债务似地，书桌上堆积着待补的笔记
给好日子笼罩上阴影
桌洞里塞着伙食费换来的口红
这是给美丽上交的那么一点点税
印染床单铺着大面积的鲜花
花丛里隐匿着蜜蜂般的机缘

床架上的长统袜很慵懒，卖弄风情
一件颜色愁苦的连衣裙月经不调
布娃娃比她的主人还出众
脸上的小雀斑古色古香
日记本暗暗地，在枕头底下怀春
一枝红杏已伸出了硬纸壳的封皮
还有刚刚封上口的信函，郑重其事得
犹如精心装修过的房间

像不爱江山爱美人一样
她们有时不爱身材爱巧克力
看书时总要吃着五香瓜子，咔嘣咔嘣
其速度与准确度超过阅读
并随时准备像嗑瓜子一样
把她们自己的身体也嗑开来
方便面吃多了怎么有股肥皂味呢
它的保质期跟爱情一样，超不过半年
而最疯狂的恋爱，也无非等于
害一场偏头痛，副产品是一大批
诗与散文，属哼哼唧唧派

时光跟口香糖般耐嚼，不见消耗
总得发生点儿什么吧，总得

从青春这朵玫瑰中提炼出点什么来

在最关健的时刻

最好是病上一场，病成西施的模样

爱情跟革命的性质相仿

往往在身心链条最薄弱的环节

取得胜利

在这里，每个人，都把自己当成

生活这部影片中的女主角

并把某男生的殷勤看成上帝发给自己的

奥斯卡奖

The Girl Students' Dormitory

in fact, a girl students' dormitory is equivalent

to a boudoir in ancient times

if they study in the Department of Chinese Language and Literature

it's more like a Xiaoxiang Guan or Hengwu Garden

the clothes and skirts, out to dry, are full of youth

coaxed as much as nourished by the sun

in the shade of the locust tree downstairs there always stands a boy

looking lost, like Jia Baoyu or Zhang Junrui

the window, with a wind bell hanging, is upheld by the pious eye

like the pagoda in the sacred revolutionary place

the last stop to love, like

an outpost position

like debts, there is a heap of pen-notes to make on the desk

that darkens the good days with shadows

desk holes stuffed with lipstick bought with meal savings

pittance of tax paid to beauty

print bed sheets spread with large acres of fresh flowers

in which serendipity hides, like bees

the stockings, over the bed rails, are lazy, ostentatiously coquettish

a dress with sad colours is in abnormal menstruation

a cloth doll is more stunning than her owner

the little speckles on its face have an antique feel

a diary, secretively, is harbouring amorous thoughts underneath the pillow

a red plum branch sticking out of its hardcover

and there is an envelope, just sealed, that looks as solemn

as a carefully furnished room

like those who love beauty more than landscape

they love chocolate more than shape

whenever they read they crack spicy melon seeds

faster and more accurate than their reading

and they are ready to crack open their bodies

the way they crack the seeds

when they have too many instant noodles they smell of soap

their shelf-life, like love, is no longer than six months

and the wildest love is no more than

suffering migraines whose side-products are

poetry and prose, of the whimpering and whingeing kind

when time, as chewy as chewing gum, is not consumed

something else must happen, something else must be extracted

from the rose that is youth

in the most critical moment

it would be best to fall ill, as ill as Xi Shi

for love, like revolution in nature

wins where the linkage is at its weakest

bodywise and heartwise

here, everyone plays the leading role herself

in the film that is life

and treats the attentions of a boy as the Oscar

God has awarded her

密苏里河畔的晚餐

面包，一块小得不能再小的农场
那是燕麦磨碎了的青春
三文鱼的脊椎已拆除，涂上一层咖喱的自信
牛肉一根筋紧绷，说不准是紧张还是刚毅
青菜叶思念沙拉成疾
米饭穿着紫菜做的寿衣

地平线吞咽着整整一条密苏里河——
水面在暮色里渐渐暗下来
我想让它替我说告别

盘子里是摆成几何图形的花园
是意象派，是静物描摹，是工笔
肠胃受到鼓励开始抒情
水杯里冰块飘浮荡漾，撞击嘴唇的客轮
一杯红酒被我高举在手上
用以唤醒身体里的自由

让密苏里河替我缓缓地说告别——

它切割着中西部平原
运载七个州的孤独，和对流逝的厌倦

女侍步履丰盈，穿白罩裙像皇后微服出行
长方形露台量走了她的青春
金属柱子上取暖灯被一盏一盏点燃
火苗中央的蓝色用力吮吸着微寒
当谈论起华尔街和经济危机
嘈杂话语里惟有元音在空气中闪烁

让密苏里河替我说告别——
在刚过去的夏天它脉管迸裂
现已恢复平静，只剩胸脯微微起伏

我佩戴五彩环饰，使脖颈显得甜蜜
心上有一个广场
痛苦在那里用足尖跳着芭蕾
白色桌面围坐了四个人
风吹起，世界需要用一个别针来固定
我的印花衬衫与对面那位先生的蓝夹克
结下了仇

让密苏里河替我说告别——

青草改了朱颜，秋天在树林上方眺望
鹰把脸朝下，它宽广的徘徊让地球略感不安

盘子空了，刀与叉不再同行
皱了的纸巾追逐着自己的末日
杯底残酒的哀愁是轻微的，没有了下文
帐单上正在签署最后一笔小费
抬头望见，不远处索桥上刚刚亮起一排灯
行李已打点好，将拖至黎明的机场

在世上不停地走，时间发出回声
哪里都可出发哪里都不是目的地
那就请密苏里河，替我缓缓地、缓缓地告别——

Dinner on the Missouri River

the bread loaf, a farm that is no smaller than itself

the grounded youth of the oats

the salmon, its spine removed, is now spread with a curry of confidence

the beef so taut with a tendon one isn't sure if it's tense or resolute

vegetable leaves are ill, missing the salad so much

and the rice, in the graveclothes of purple laver

the horizon is swallowing up the Missouri River—

its water surface darkening in the dusk

I'd prefer that it take farewell for me

a garden in the plate, in the shape of geometry

is imagist, the delineation of a still life, a worked brush

the stomach, encouraged, is turning lyrical

ice cubes, in the glass, are floating, smashing against the liner of my lips

a glass of red wine, raised high in my hand

is awakening the freedom of my body

let the Missouri take its slow farewell for me—

as it cuts through the Midwest Plains

carrying the loneliness of seven states and its weariness with the passage

the waitress walks in plump steps, in a white gown that looks like an
    empress in plain clothes
the oblong patio measuring her youth
the heating lamp, on the metal piles, are lit one after another
the blue in the centre of the flame is sucking the cold strenuously
and when they talk about Wall Street and the financial crisis
only the consonants in the noise shine in the air

let the Missouri take farewell for me—
in the summer just gone, its haemal tube went bust
now, peace recovered, its chest is gently heaving

I wear an annulet, of five colours, that makes my neck sweet
there is a square in my heart
where pain is ballet-dancing on tiptoes
a white table, surrounded by four
when the wind blows, the world needs a safety pin to fix
but my print blouse is becoming enemies with the blue jacket
of the gentleman sitting opposite me

I'll let the Missouri take farewell for me—
when the grass changes its colour, the autumn watching over the forest
the eagle, face down, paces so expansively the earth feels slightly uneasy

the plates empty, the forks and the knives no longer walking together

the crumpled tissues chasing their own end

the sadness in the remaining wine is tiny, nothing to follow

and the final tip is being signed for the bill

as I raise my head, I see a row of lights lit on the cable bridge nearby

luggage ready, to be hauled towards the dawn airport

I keep walking on the world, time echoing time

one can begin anywhere but arrives nowhere

still, let the Missouri take a slow, very slow farewell for me—

小南风

小南风把我吹得头晕
春天说来就来了么
我血管奔突，骨缝松动
从头到脚无比绵软
心是全身结出的唯一的果子

真不知道这春天的压强是多少
即每平方厘米的皮肤负载多少吨敏感和灵犀
那延续多年的日常生活已经坍塌
得需要几倍的麻木和平庸才能重新支撑起来

阳光散发出新鲜的膏药味
那是紧紧封闭又忽然打开的气味
连尘土都显得芬芳起来
薄薄的红夹袄裹着小而鼓的身躯
敲击地面的双脚像两只小槌
每一秒钟都不能浪费
全都用来什么也不做
其成果是建造起一座空中楼阁

小南风吹呀吹

它吹着它所热爱的这个春天

吹着这个春天里最幸福的人

吹着这个人发辫上黄绿相间的头绳

吹着头绳末端温润的小圆坠儿

小南风吹呀吹

它自己已分不清东西南北

The Southern Breeze

the southern breeze is making me dizzy

has the spring come just like that?

my blood vessels are running, the seams of my bones loosening

turning soft from head to toe

my heart the only fruit borne by my body

how do I know the intensity of pressure of this spring?

that is: how many tons of sensitivity and spirit every centimetre of my skin

      bears

the ordinary life, having been continuing for years, has now collapsed

many folds of numbness and mediocrity are needed to prop it up again

the sun is sending forth a fresh smell of plaster

the smell suddenly released after tightly sealing

even the dust seems fragrant

a red padded jacket wrapping up my body, small and swelling

my feet that knock on the ground resemble wooden mallets

not a single second is to be wasted

to be used to do nothing

but create a pagoda in the air

the southern breeze is blowing

across the spring it is in love with

the happiest person in this spring

the hair band of yellow and green in this person's plait

and the warm, round pendant at the end of the band

the southern breeze keeps blowing

blowing in all directions without itself knowing it

小睡

穿堂风布置了这一切。
你在大屋睡着了，我躺在隔壁小屋里
静静地想你。
我拥着薄被，上面有笨拙的温柔
亲爱的棉花在里面轻轻喘息

相隔一尺，我的南墙就是你的北墙
我的呼吸与你的鼾声押韵
韵脚轻轻拍打着
一面薄薄的墙

我知道这个初夏的中午爱我
它用床单上的方格子爱我
它用蓬松的树冠
和飘摇的裙裾爱我
还有爬山虎正在窗外的墙上蔓延
那是它爱我的最好方式

我感到安稳。

身体有点迷糊和无知，正满足地下坠

我知道我会梦见你，以及整个北方

Taking a Nap

the drought has arranged everything here.
you are asleep in the big room and I, lying down in the little one next door
quietly thinking of you.
I am covered with a thin quilt, with clumsy tenderness
inside which dear cotton is gently breathing

a foot between us, my southern wall is your northern
my breathing rhyming with your snoring
the rhyming feet gently patting
a thin wall

I know this early summer noon loves me
it loves me with the bed sheet with squares
it loves me, too, with the fluffy treetops
and the flapping skirts
the mountain-climbing tiger creepers are spreading on the wall outside the
        window
the best way it loves me

I feel at peace and at ease

my body a little dazed and ignorant, sinking with satisfaction

I know I shall dream of you, and of the whole north

尼姑庵

生活也像这庵堂一样

每天跟任何一天没什么不同

一辈子还没有过就要结束

门前的花开了又落，落了又开

屋后的树绿了又黄，黄了又绿

连一株小草也摇曳着她的时装

可是我呢，永远是青砖灰瓦的颜色

骨髓里的香气因长期囚禁而变质发霉

我被禁锢在一个小小壁龛里

欲望和道德非法共眠，互相吞食着内脏

暮鼓晨钟把每个白天和黑夜处决

那些断气的美好假日像在春天就被连根拔起的玫瑰

永远不会相信复活

经书有一副棺材铺的外表，以及口琴般处处是孔的心计

其厚度刚好能够把轻快的步履绊倒在地

我活着，却已和生命分手

性情比那面锈着的山崖还要荒僻

身体比枯死的树枝还要严肃

表情还不如一块青石板，连苔藓都不生
甚至，在我映衬着田野的空空臂弯里
根本感觉不到空气存在

可是，一只时空时满的水罐，不知是为什么
里面映出的总是一张许多年前的脸
用火焰镶嵌的笑容如一个从尘世匿迹的密语
在水中闪闪烁烁
那哑默的木鱼在悲伤
想找一个被敲响的时刻还原，从水中游走
你看，梦的酵母从来不需太多
只要有了那么一丁点儿，就可以使心鼓胀起来
某种念头像白炽灯泡，像成群吱吱狙狙尖叫的耗子
从寂静奔向寂静，在南墙上反弹回不祥的回音

我多么羡慕窗前那束杏花，朝生夕死
魂魄像一块白绢那么温柔
我不知爱情是什么，不曾写过甜言蜜语
但我将留下遗书
我的遗嘱会像私生子那样隐蔽，石破天惊

The Nunnery

life, like this nunnery

has days that are no different from one another

it ends even before it is lived

the flowers outside open and fall, and fall and open

the trees behind the house green and yellow, and yellow and green

even a small grass flashes her fashion

but I, the colour of blue brick and grey tile

deteriorate and go moldy because of the long imprisonment of the aroma

    in my bone marrow

locked inside a tiny niche

I, illegally, sleep with desire and morality, swallowing each other's innards

the drum and evening bell execute days and nights

the beautiful holidays, that have breathed their last, resemble the roses,

    uprooted in the spring

never believing in resurrection

the classics look like a coffin shop, as calculating as a mouth organ, punched

    everywhere with holes

its thickness just enough to trip the lightest steps

I live but I have parted company with life

my character more desolate than the embroidered cliff

my body more serious than the dead branches

my expression no better than a slate of bluestone, where no moss gathers

and, in the hollow of my arms that reflects the fields

one feels the non-existence of air

however, a jug, sometimes empty and sometimes full, somehow shows

a face many years ago

its smile, framed with fire, like a secret code that erases its traces from the

      dusty world

flickers in the water

the mute wooden fish is sorrowing

and, looking for the recovery of knocked time, intends to swim away

look, the yeast of dream needs little

to swell the heart

an idea, like an incandescent bulb, rushes from quietude

to quietude, like screaming rats, an ominous sound bouncing back from the

      southern wall

how I admire the bunch of plum flowers by the window, born in the

      morning and dying at dusk

its soul as tender as a white handkerchief

I do not know what love is; I have not written honeyed words

but I shall keep a post-life letter

and my will, will one day break the sky, as hidden as an illegitimate child

我回来了

我回来了。

一只蚂蚁绕地球一圈

驮着两大箱子的想法，一路留下不浅不深的车辙

一只燕子飞过四个温度带

体内的小小发动机不停，微微发烫

在心中记下南北东西的景色。

我回来了，回来了

钥匙还是那一把，铜的，柄上有一点缺口

末端的圆孔拴了红黄相间的头绳

我用它打开久闭的积尘的木门

插上所有电源，给灯泡电脑洗衣机冰箱和空调

都输入进温暖的血液

多么好，我重新听到了这幢房屋的脉搏。

我回来了，挂历上的鸢尾还在开着

北墙上那簇上百年的荷兰向日葵

依然在等待收割

纯棉床单上不多不少，还是印着122个方格。

一只蜘蛛在门后的墙角安了家

两只年轻的蛾子从大米袋子里飞出

结伴而行，从厨房飞到后凉台去郊游

三只棕色小蟑螂亮亮的，趴在灰色地板上佯装缄默。
是的，我和我的偏头疼一起回来了
我和我那一肚子发霉的汉字，一起回来了
我和一个国家被雨淋湿的千里暮色一起回来了
没有胖也没有瘦，心里还是流淌着一条大河
头上的发卡还是那一个，项链上的小石头还是那一颗
啊真的，真的没有改变什么
只是比从前多带回了
一本世界地图册

I Am Back

I am back

an ant that has encircled the earth

carrying two big suitcases of thoughts, leaving ruts not deep or shallow

a swallow across four zones of temperature

its body-engine unstoppable, slightly heated up

the landscapes recorded in the heart of south, north, east and west

I am back, and I am back

the key is the same old one, copper, a gap on its handle

the hole at the end tied with a hair-binding string in red and yellow

with which I open the wooden door, closed for a long time, gathering dust

I plug in all electricity for bulbs, the computer, the washing machine, the

     refrigerator and the air-conditioner

putting warm blood into all of them

it feels so good when I hear, once again, the pulse of this house

I am back. The iris is still in bloom on the wall calendar

and, on the northern wall, the bunch of Dutch sun flowers, more than a

     hundred years old

are still waiting for harvesting

the pure cotton bed sheet is printed with 122 squares, no more, no less

a spider has taken residence in a corner behind the door

two young moths are flying from out of the rice bag

in company, out the kitchen, to take a stroll on the back balcony three tiny brown cockroaches, shiny, and crouching on the grey floor,

      pretend to be quiet

yes, my migraine has returned with me

I have returned with a bellyful of moldy Chinese characters

and with a nation's thousand kilometres of dusk wetted with rain

not thinner or fatter, still a big river flowing in my heart

my hairpin remains the same, and the stone on my necklace also the same

ah, it is true that nothing much else has changed

the only thing extra that I've brought back

is a world map

我想去看你

用红笔标示出所有
能到达你的城市的车次和航班
我想去看你，我想

心在风里向西飘上几千里
中国的版图广大得多么奢侈
支撑得起最丰富的想象
这些铁路和航线
都是为我这次远行而修筑和开通的

我想去看你
我很贫穷
从今天开始要省吃俭用
攒足去你那里的盘缠

我是一个卑微的人
但你要像迎接文成公主一样
迎接我
在当年她驻足的地方
请为我接风洗尘

她西去的目的是和亲
我的目的是挑起一场温柔的战争

要选择一个好日子
海陆空畅通无阻
头脑保持最简单状态
行李就是我这个人
我要开小差
从灰黯的生活里悄悄溜走
我不会告诉任何人我去了哪里

我要去看你
看你一眼就回来
从此以后死心塌地
埋下头，继续孤孤单单
一天一天苟活下去

I'd Like to Go and See You

tracing all the train numbers and flights

with a red pen

I'd like to go and see you, I'd like to

my heart, in the wind, is drifting westward for thousands of kilometres

the map of China so extravagantly vast

that it can support the richest imagination

all these railways and flight routes

have been constructed and opened for my long journey

I'd love to go and see you

I am poor

but, from today onwards, I'll save up

enough money to cover my journey to you

although I am petty and low

you must receive me like Princess Wencheng

and you must receive me

where she once stayed

and welcome me with wind-receiving and dust-washing

she went west to make peace

as I do, to provoke a tender war

I must choose a good day

when there is no obstruction by sea, by land or by air

when my mind is kept at its simplest

and when my luggage is I, myself

I shall desert

slipping away from my grey life

I shall tell no one where I am going

I would like to go and see you

just to take a single look at you before I come back

I shall then keep my head down

laying my heart low and remaining single

living on in degradation

打棺材

打棺材的人在忙碌
死亡是新鲜的
带着木屑和刨花的清香
刚刚死去的外公躺在屋里
我相信他一定听到了
外面锯木头砸钉子的声音

同时我感到
空气中有朵大白花在悄悄开放

阳光普照，显得很阔绰
我在庭院里走来走去
我、还、活、着、
五脏六腑完好
渴望寻欢作乐，唯恋爱是图

我希望打棺材的动静尽量轻一些
我不愿让屋里那个人听到
这不吉利的响声
他说不定会因此生气

也许他以为自己只是在小睡
过会儿就会醒来
推开窗户仰起头
朝着天空看看风向

空气中有朵大白花
在悄悄开放

我考虑着
往棺材里放什么
录音机和吕剧磁带
舒喘灵气雾剂、还有布老虎
一顶呢帽子和假牙
要放的东西实在多
我不想把那个人放进去了

空气中那朵大白花
开得越来越大越来越轻

Making a Coffin

people were busy making a coffin

death was fresh

with a clear fragrance of wood chips and shavings

my grandfather, just dead, lay inside the house

he, I believe, must have heard

the sawing of the wood and the hammering of the nails outside

at the same time when I felt

that there was a large white flower opening, quietly, in the air

the sunlight everywhere, seemingly generous enough

I was walking in the courtyard

I, was, still, alive,

my viscera intact

desiring to seek pleasure, for love alone

the makers of the coffin, I was hoping, should reduce the noise to a
        minimum

as I did not want the person inside the house to hear this

unlucky noise

he might have got upset

perhaps he was only assuming that he was taking a nap

and would wake up in a little while

when he would push the window open and raise his head
towards the sky in order to observe the direction of the wind

there was a large white flower
opening, quietly, in the air

I was wondering what
to place inside the coffin
a tape-recorder with a tape of Lü Opera
an asthma gas spray, a cloth tiger
a woolen hat and a set of dentures
there were just so many to put in
I didn't want to include the person

the large white flower in the air
was becoming larger, and lighter

晚安

晚安——

当我们彼此这样说的时候

电话线在风中轻轻地荡了一个弯

我楼下的茑萝早就合上了眼睑

你屋外的水菖蒲用外省口音打起轻鼾

我们相隔的上千平方公里啊

在半明半暗中笼罩着淡雾和轻烟

晚安——

这两个字的韵脚可用来催眠

使心跳和血流慢下来，使骨骼里的钙积淀

使大脑像广场那样空，使我的子宫像花骨朵那样饱满

在黑暗中消除着疲倦

晚安——

梦这只蚕很快就咬破躯壳和棉被这两层茧，从中飞出

而那些还没来得及飞走的

会把填满谷糠的枕头沉沉地压扁

晚安——，晚安——

一条大河和一条大江的中下游平原连成一片

被我们当成大床
在上面手拉着手一起入眠

Good Night

good night—

when we said it to each other

the telephone line waved a gentle curve in the wind

my cypress vine downstairs having closed its eyelids

and your rhizoma acori calami outside were snoring in a provincial accent

the thousand-square-kilometres that separated us

were shrouded in a thin mist and smoke, in semi-darkness

good night—

the rhyme of the two words could serve as a lullaby

slowing down the heartbeats and blood flow and helping the calcium in the
    bones deposit

making the brains as deserted as a square and filling my womb like a
    flower bud

lessening the fatigue in the darkness

good night—

soon, the silkworms of dream would bite through the body and quilt of the
    cocoon, to fly out

and those who had yet to fly away

would heavily flatten the pillow, filled with grain husks

good night—

good night—

the middle and lower reaches now joined of two big rivers

treating us like a huge bed

on which to go into sleep, hand in hand

江堤

在日落时分走上江堤
走上这个小岛环抱着的长臂
臂外是千里江水
臂弯里拢着满满的青草和花，散落其间的房屋多么安宁
那些低首劳作的人，把远远的天空当作誓言
在认真地刺绣着大地

在我的一生中，有这样一个黄昏
和你一起走在这大堤上
风从背后轻轻抱住我们
被脚步声惊动的麻雀，像雀斑那样点点飞起之后
留下了那些沉默的芦苇
当走到大堤拐弯处，在这小岛荒凉的肘部
江面的落日已成为世界的中心，巨大的寂静
压迫着我和你的呼吸

The River Bank

I took to the river bank at dusk

walking onto the long arm embracing this isle

outside the arm, a river running thousands of *li*

inside it, a full hug of grass and flowers, with scattered houses so peaceful

    and quiet

the labouring people, their heads lowered, took the distant skies as a

    warning

and were embroidering the land in earnest

there once was such a dusk in my life

when I, with you, walked onto this great bank

the wind, gently, hugging us from behind

the sparrows, startled by our footsteps, took flight like speckles

leaving the silent reeds where they were

when we reached the bend of the bank, at the deserted elbow of the isle

the setting sun on the river had become the centre of the world, a huge

    quietness

oppressing the breathings, of mine, and yours

素食主义者

只挑带禾木旁、米字旁、草字头和木字旁的来吃
名词经过食道的引擎，会演变成动词
一定是环保的、和平的动词

我的牙齿温良恭俭让，我的舌头悲天悯人
我的肠胃天人合一
我的身体天涯何处无芳草
我从头到脚就是一部本草纲目

我的皮肤是小麦和稻谷的颜色，脖子荸荠白
发型是韭菜倒垂、海带盘起、雪里蕻披散开来
倘如我是男人，就以豌豆苗为胡须
我的四肢是莲藕做成的
在甘蔗的脊骨和芹菜的肋骨之下
心脏是一只洋葱头，肠道是长长的豆角
还有香菇的肝、大白菜叶的肺、西红柿的肾和土豆形的胃
一粒花生是那没用的阑尾
我有圆锥形竹笋肚子、南瓜臀和丝瓜腰
乳房是两个白色花椰菜，生殖器是仲夏的带籽的莲蓬

而脸是水果：椰子的脸盘、芒果的额头、苹果的双颊
草莓鼻子、樱桃嘴、菱角耳朵、葡萄眼睛
而目光是切开来的甜橙
右下颌的痣如同一粒小小桑椹

我的革命手段是温柔
我的哲学是非暴力，我的道德是平等
我穿着胡萝卜缨子的T恤和荷叶的短裙
向所有哺乳动物、爬行动物、鸟类、鱼类和昆虫
致以人类的崇高敬意——

A Vegan

eating only those with radicals signifying grain, rice, grass and wood

nouns, when passing through the engine of esophagus, turn into verbs

that must be ecological and peaceful

my teeth are temperate and courteous, my tongue, compassionate

my stomach and intestines, a combination of woman with heaven

my body is covered with fragrant grass everywhere

and I am a *Compendium of Materia Medica*, from head to toe

my skin the colour of wheat and rice, my neck as white as *chufa*

my hairstyle like Chinese chive, hanging upside down, curled like seaweed,

    and sweeping like potherb mustard

if I were a man, I'd use bean sprout as my moustache

my limbs made of lotus-roots

beneath the bones of sugar cane and the ribs of celery

the heart is an onion bulb and the intestines, long kidney beans

there are also livers of mushroom, lungs of celery cabbage, kidneys of

    tomatoes and a stomach shaped like a potato

a peanut is the useless appendix

and I have a belly shaped like a coned bamboo shoot, hips of pumpkin and

    a waist like a sponge gourd

my breasts two white cauliflowers and my private parts, a seedpod of the
     lotus in mid-summer
and my face fruit: coconut for the cast of my face, mango for forehead and
     apple for cheeks
strawberry for nose, cherry for lips, water caltrop for ears, grapes for eyes
and the way I look is a sweet orange, cut open
and the mole, on my lower right chin, is like the tiny seed of a mulberry

my revolutionary measure is tenderness
my philosophy is non-violence and my moral is equality
I wear a T-shirt with radish leaves and a shirt skirt with lotus-leaves
and I pay the highest human respect to all the mammals
reptiles, birds, fish and insects—

肯登镇

我一个人来到肯登镇
我要去瓦尔特·惠特曼的家
我看见遍地时代的草叶，命运的涂鸦

我一个人来到肯登镇
永恒的太阳照耀马丁·路德·金大道
大西洋起伏，跟我一起朗诵："我听见美国在歌唱"
声音传送得多么广大

我一个人来到肯登镇
红砖楼的山墙上涂抹着粗糙的水泥
是贫穷的青色加上落魄的灰色
四周脏乱差，这是我热爱的诗人的家

我一个人来到肯登镇
门锁着，不见那个粗野又文雅的男人
透过窗子可望见空空的摇椅
这个寂静的晌午，我坐在他门前的台阶上
对房前两棵枫树说："我写诗，来自中国，八里洼。"

我怀揣两个洲的孤独和一根琴弦，一个人来到肯登镇
我头顶三万里南风，沿着分行的道路，来到肯登镇
在我那同样带电的肉体里
英语单词在发芽，汉字在吐穗、在开花

Camden

alone, I arrived at Camden

where I'd like to visit Walt Whitman's home

I could see the grass and leaves all over the place, graffiti of fate

alone, I arrived at Camden

the eternal sun shining on Martin Luther King Avenue

the Atlantic Ocean heaving, reading aloud with me, 'I hear America

     singing'

the voice carrying so vast

alone, I arrived at Camden

the gable on the red-brick building smeared with rough cement

black colour of poverty and, grey, of a lost soul

such messy surroundings but it's the home of a poet I love

alone, I arrived at Camden

the door under lock and key, where I did not see the man wild but elegant

through the window, I could see the empty rocking chair

on this quiet noon, I sat on his front steps

and said to the two maple trees: I write poetry, from Baliwa, China carrying the solitude of two continents and a musical string, I arrived,

  alone, at Camden

a southern wind of thirty thousand *li* on my head, I, through divided lines,

  arrived at Camden

in my body likewise electrified

the English words were germinating as the Chinese characters were in the

  ear, flowering

镜子

一面从未照过的镜子最透明
其内部的时间是凝固着的
它盲目、寒冷、空旷，像处女
只有风在流连顾盼
在里面照映着某种空想
其实，这时候的镜子还不是镜子

使镜子真正成为镜子的
该是一个充满期翼与忧伤的女人
她在岁月的躯体里种植豌豆或蔷薇
以白日梦替代什么也不是的生活
她有这么一面挂在墙上的心扉
美丽的隐私使平面玻璃充实起来
表情像汉语一样闪烁歧义和双关

镜子是可以拷贝的软盘
往它的最深层遥望
一长串多年贮存的映像呈透视效果
排成一条幽长幽长的隧道
初春的嫩绿一定会变成深秋的枯黄

无论多么衰老，这女人都可以穿透镜子
沿隧道返回青春年少的时光
在那里，她依然眼眸如星
黑发永远拖在脑后，像泛滥的柔情

镜子是她的信仰，她的乌托邦
今生与她最相爱的，不是别人
而是囚禁在镜中的那一个
两个女人如此对称地
栖居在不同的深渊里
连光阴也被复制出蒙蒙的影子
无数瞬间在镜中重重叠叠
成为同一瞬间

镜面蒙尘，那叫遗忘
如果镜子出现裂痕
那是命运遇上了劫数
心撕裂过才知道什么叫沧桑
如果镜子彻底摔碎
那就是一个宇宙遭到了毁灭
那样的碎片真的不亚于一场号啕

The Mirror

a mirror one never looks into remains the most transparent

the time inside it being frozen

blind, cold and empty, like a virgin

it has only wind lingering

with a utopian idea reflected within it

whereas, in fact, it is not a mirror that is a mirror

what makes the mirror a mirror

must be a woman filled with expectancy and sorrow

who grows peas or roses in the body of time

replacing a life that is nothing with daydreams

she has such a mirror, a heart-door, hanging on the wall

whose beautiful secrets enrich the plane glass

and whose facial expression is equivocal, with double meanings, in Chinese

the mirror can be a floppy disk

if you look into its depths

a long series of reflections, stored for years, present perspective effects

in a secluded long tunnel

where tender green of an early spring is sure to turn into withered yellow

    of a deep autumn

however aged, this woman can return, via the tunnel

and through the mirror, to her youthful years

there, her eyes are still starry

and her hair behind her, in a flood of love

the mirror is what she believes in, her utopia

this life, the one, who loves her best, is not anyone else

but the one imprisoned in the mirror

the two women, so symmetrical

take residence in different abysses

even time has been duplicated in hazy shadows

countless instants overlapping themselves in the mirror

becoming the same instant

when the mirror is covered in dust, it is forgetfulness

if the mirror cracks

it is fate meeting with inexorable doom

the heart, when ripped apart, knows what is vicissitudes

and if the mirror breaks into pieces

it is a universe destroyed

its fragments no less than a wail

阳台上

站在阳台上就能望见长江是幸福的
目光越过的那些树梢和荷塘，也是幸福的
你站在我身边，我的心因幸福
而变得昏沉

整个江心洲，没有一棵树不会做诗
整个江心洲，没有一朵花不会谈情说爱
我们的细语要尽量放得低些，以免让它们听见

一幢从阳台上能看见长江的房子
再简朴都称得上是豪宅
窗子朝六月敞开，夏天的五脏六腑露了出来
我身体里的那个夏天也正值水草丰茂
单单向着你打开

另有一条长江从我的心脏出发，流遍全身
哦，我的心脏是源头各拉丹冬

血脉蜿蜒6300公里，分上游中游下游
还有，在最温柔的地方
也有一个江心洲

On the Balcony

it is pure happiness to be able to see the Yangtze while standing on the
    balcony
it is also pure happiness to be able to see those treetops and lotus ponds
with you standing by my side, my heart is so happy
it feels dizzy

on the sandbar in the heart of the river, there is not a tree that cannot make
    poetry
on the sandbar in the heart of the river, there is not a flower that cannot
    talk love
we must whisper in a still lower voice, lest they may overhear it

a house from whose balcony one can see the Yangtze
can be called a luxury residence even at its humblest
my windows all open towards June and the viscera of the summer exposed
the summer in my body happens to be lush with water grass
open only for you

there is another Yangtze that originates in my heart, running through my
    body
ah, my heart is the origin of Mount Geladaindong

my veins meandering for 6300 kilometres, with upper, middle and lower
    reaches

and, at its tenderest place

there is also a sandbar in the heart of the river

山间坟茔

去往东南诸峰途中，遇一座旧坟
枯草掩映着它不知哪朝哪代的面颊
一个土包、一块断碑、两块条石
把死亡均摊

春节前夕，坟上刚刚压了姜黄色的冥纸
使得悲伤又被刷新
让经过者看清所有英雄的末路
弄明白在一个坏了的宇宙里不会有好风水

里面或许点着一盏油灯，里面或许有打不开的网络链接
那人或许还在等一个口信
四周的时间在返回，空气充满预感

一片开阔地留给了晌午的阳光
松鼠跳到墓碑上方的树枝，瞅着碑文
双拳相抱，求签问卜

我走近了，那被两三行碑文紧紧关闭在里面的人
试图文白夹杂

说服外面这个病得不轻的人
话语全都写在了风上

春天来时，里面的纵声大笑会透过变松变软的土层
传递出来
在它的左前方，桃花感动山涧流水

走远之后，在一段上坡路
又回头瞭望这座小坟
我瞥见孤独的源头
天地悠悠，每秒钟都正在变成灰烬

A Grave in the Mountain

on my way to the peaks in the Southeast, I came across a grave

its face of an unknown dynasty, concealed by the withered grass

a mound, a broken gravestone and two ashlars

had an equal share of death amongst them

on Chinese New Year's Eve, the grave was newly covered with

ginger-coloured paper hell money, updating the old sorrow

for the passers-by to see the dead end of all the heroes and understand that
     there

wouldn't be any good *fengshui* in a corrupted universe

there might have been an oil lamp, lit in there, or webpages that refused to

open as the person might have been waiting for a spoken message

all around, time, though, was returning, the air filled with premonition

in an open ground, left for the noon sun

a sparrow leapt to a branch over the grave, staring at the inscription

its claws folded and raised in front of its face, as if in prayer

as I approached, the person, tightly enclosed with the inscribed lines

tried to persuade the one so sick outside

in a language mixing the vernacular with the literary

all the words written in a wind

when spring came, screams of laughter would burst out through the
    softened and loosened soil
and, to its left in the front, peach flowers would move the mountain
    streams

after I went afar, on the section of a slope
I turned to watch that small grave
and saw, in one glance, the source of solitude
every second was turning into ashes between heaven and earth

山垭

我在一个山垭停了下来
两簇峰峦之间的这个路口
背向不远处一座倒塌的古寺
胸襟朝东敞开，去往山下一个小村

我在一个山垭口停下来
山的册页被我哗哗乱翻，至此打开新篇
是一只豆雁把我引到这里
它飞得没了踪影之后，我仍然望着空中出神

我在这个山垭停下
一个农妇孤坐避风的崖根，向我兜售黑枣
它们盛在布袋里，肉少籽多，长相贫寒
吸取了尘土的味道
它们安慰过我的童年，现在又来安慰一个失败者的内心

我在这个山垭停下来
这是两道山脊延伸并渐渐靠近之后
尾骨衔接之处

我想在地图上标注这个垭口，给它起个名字
我想听到自己的回声

我在这样一个山垭停下来
有一朵云恰好也飘到了这里
它看上去没有力气，形状像有了身孕
它继续往前移动时，我向它挥手告别
彼此相忘

我在一个山垭停下来
天色渐晚，黄昏有一个巨大的门槛

The Mountain Pass

I stopped at a mountain pass
the mouth of a road between the two clusters of peaks
at the back of a fallen ancient temple, not far off
and I faced east, on my way down to another small village

I stopped at the mouth of a mountain pass
as I noisily turned its pages, opening up a new chapter
it was a bean goose that had guided me here
where I was watching the skies after it's gone, leaving not a trace

I stopped at this mountain pass
where a peasant woman sat alone at the foot of a sheltering cliff, selling
    black dates to
me, from a sack, dates with more seeds than flesh, looking poor, having
    absorbed the
taste of dust and comforted me
in my childhood, they now came to comfort the heart of one who had
    failed

I stopped at this mountain pass
where the tailbones of the two ridges linked up after they extended
and gradually got closer

I would like to mark this pass on a map and give it a name
for I'd like to hear my own echoes

I stopped at such a mountain pass
and a cloud happened to have also drifted here
looking powerless, in the shape of a seeming pregnancy
as it started moving ahead, I waved my farewell to it
we, forgetting each other

I stopped at a mountain pass
as it was getting late, there was a huge threshold at dusk

月出东山

月出东山，又大又圆
照耀着归途，我像一首诗那样
拐弯并折行
从山顶渐渐下来

天地正吱吱嘎嘎关闭大门，四周多么寂静
屏住呼吸，才能听到山间细语
今夜盛大月光要把世界映成一个剧院
农历十五，月亮在她的排卵期
无比饱满

柏树林勾勒出来的山际线
色泽也在一层一层加深
一只披黑斗篷穿白衬衣的大鸟
从草丛跃起，飞进暮色
我加快了脚步

山脚下的灯火在望
我的心已比我这个人先到了家
忽然，一只刺猬披着铁蒺藜拦在路上

它说：你好
并且想给我一个大大的拥抱

Moon Over the Eastern Hills

the moon, huge and round, over the eastern hills
shone on my return journey, on which I, like a poem
made a turn and bent
coming down from the top, slowly

heaven and earth were closing their gates, with a creaking noise, so quiet
all around that I had to hold my breath to hear the whisper of the hills
moonlight tonight, so spectacular, was turning the world into a theatre
on the 15th of the lunar calendar, the moon, in her ovulatory period
was incomparably round

the tinctures of the mountain line, delineated by the cypress
forest, were deepening layer by layer
a big bird, in a black cape and white shirt
leapt from the grass and flew into the evening
as I quickened my footsteps

the glow at the foot of the hill in sight
my heart, though, had rushed home ahead of me
when a hedgehog, covered with barbed wire, stopped me on the road

and said: How are you

intending to give me a big hug

山上

我跟随着你。这个黄昏我多么欢喜
整个这座五月的南山
就是我想对你说出的话
为了表达自己，我想变成野菊
开成一朵又一朵

我跟随着你。我不看你
也知道你的辽阔
风吹过山下的红屋顶
仰望天空，横贯南北的白色雾线
那是一架飞机的苦闷

我跟随着你。心窸窸簌簌
是野兔在灌木丛里躲闪
松树耸着肩膀
去年的松果掉到了地上

我跟随着你。紫槐寂静
蜜蜂停在它的柱形花上
细小的苦楝叶子很像我的发卡

时光很快就会过去

成为草丛里一块墓碑，字迹模糊

我跟随着你

你牵引我误入幽深的山谷

天色渐晚，袭来的花香多么昏暗

大青石发出古老的叹息

在这里我看见了

我的故国我的前生

On a Hill

I followed you. I was so delighted this evening
the whole of this southern hill in May
was the words I'd love to say to you
to express myself, I'd love to turn myself into a wild chrysanthemum
one after another

I followed you. I did not look at you
and I knew you were vast
when the wind swept across the red rooftops down the hill
I looked up at the skies and knew that the white fog line interconnecting
      the South and
the North was the dejection of an airplane

I followed you. My heart rustling
was a wild rabbit that hid itself in a bush
while a pine tree was shrugging its shoulders
pinecones of last year fell onto the ground

I followed you. The purple Chinese scholartree was so quiet
that bees were perched on its column-shaped flowers
the tiny leaves of a Chinaberry tree resembled my hairpin
and time would soon pass
becoming a gravestone in the cluster of grasses, with faint inscriptions

I followed you

and was wrongly led by you into a deep valley

it was getting late and the fragrance of the flowers came with such

     darkness

the great bluestone sighed an ancient sigh

where I could see

my previous life in the country of my birth

木梳

我带上一把木梳去看你
在年少轻狂的南风里
去那个有你的省，那座东经118度北纬32度的城。
我没有百宝箱，只有这把桃花心木梳子
梳理闲愁和微微的偏头疼。
在那里，我要你给我起个小名
依照那些遍种的植物来称呼我：
梅花、桂子、茉莉、枫杨或者菱角都行
她们是我的姐妹，前世的乡愁。
我们临水而居
身边的那条江叫扬子，那条河叫运河
还有一个叫瓜洲的渡口
我们在雕花木窗下
吃莼菜和鲈鱼，喝碧螺春与糯米酒
写出使洛阳纸贵的诗
在棋盘上谈论人生
用一把轻摇的丝绸扇子送走恩怨情仇。
我常常想就这样回到古代，进入水墨山水

过一种名叫沁园春或如梦令的幸福生活

我是你云鬓轻挽的娘子，你是我那断了仕途的官人。

A Wooden Comb

I went to visit you, with a wooden comb

in the southern wind that was young and wild

to that province, with you in it, that city, 32 degrees north latitude, and 118
   degrees east longitude.

I had no treasure box except this comb, made of peach-flower-heart wood

to comb away my leisurely concerns and my slight migraine.

there, I'd like you to give me a pet name

in accordance with the widely grown plants:

plum flowers, laurel blossoms, jasmine, maple, and even water caltrop

as they were my sisters from, and, my nostalgia for, a previous life.

we lived by the water

the one next to us was the Yangtze and the other, the Canal

and there's also a ferry, called the Melon Sandbar

where we sat by the carved wooden window

eating the water shield and a perch while drinking Biluo Spring tea and
   glutinous rice

wine, producing poetry that would have made it

expensive to buy

and talking about life while playing a chess game

waving all the rancour off, gently with a silken fan.

that's the way I often think of going back to the ancient times

to enter into the ink-and-wash mountains and waters

and lead a happy life, called 'Qinyuan Spring' or 'Dream-like Ling'

I, your woman with her cloudy hair lightly lifted, and you, my man with your official career at an end.

火车站

它的人群苍茫，它的站台颤动

它的发烫的铁轨上蜿蜒着全部命运

它的步梯和天桥运载一个匆忙的时代

它的大钟发出告别的回声

它的尖顶之上的天空多么高多么远，对应遥遥里程

它的整个建筑因太多离愁别恨而下沉

它的昏暗的地下道口钻出了我这个蓬头垢面的人

身后行李箱的轮子在方块砖上滚过

发出青春最后的轰轰隆隆的响声

The Railway Station

its crowds that were vast, its platform that was shivering

its hot rails that meandered with all the fate

its steps and overpasses that conveyed a busy time

its big clock that echoed the farewell

its sky above its steeple that was so high and far, matching the miles

its whole building that was sinking with too many a sad departure

its dark underground exit from which emerged I, unkempt

the wheels of my suitcase rolling behind me across the brick-cube

      pavement

sending forth a rumbling noise of my remaining youth

江心洲

给出十年时间
我们到江心洲上去安家
一个像首饰盒那样小巧精致的家

江心洲是一条大江的合页
江水在它的北边离别又在南端重逢
我们初来乍到，手拉着手
绕岛一周

在这里我称油菜花为姐姐芦蒿为妹妹
向猫和狗学习自由和单纯
一只蚕伏在桑叶上，那是它的祖国
在江南潮润的天空下
我还来得及生育
来得及像种植一畦豌豆那样
把儿女养大

把床安放在窗前
做爱时可以越过屋外的芦苇塘和水杉树
看见长江

远方来的货轮用笛声使我们的身体
摆脱地心引力

我们志向宏伟，赶得上这里的造船厂
把豪华想法藏在锈迹斑斑的劳作中
每天面对着一条大江居住
光住也能住成李白

我要改编一首歌来唱
歌名叫《我的家在江心洲上》
下面一句应当是"这里有我亲爱的某某"

Sandbar in the Heart of the River

give me ten years

and we shall settle down on the sandbar in the heart of the river

in a home as small and delicate as a jewelry box

the river-heart sandbar acts like a hinge in the river

as the water departs in its north and has a reunion at its southern end

we circled the island

hand in hand when we first arrived

here, I called canola flowers my older sisters and I called Artemisia

      selengensis my younger sisters

I learnt freedom and simplicity from cats and dogs

a silkworm was lying on a mulberry leaf as it was its motherland

under the moist sky of River South

I still had time to give birth

and to bring up kids

the way one plants and grows a plot of peas

I'd like to put my bed before the window

where we could, while making love, see the Yangtze

across the reed pond and through the dawn redwood

when the siren of a cargo ship in the distance would rid our bodies

of the gravity

we had great ambitions that would match those of a shipyard here

and we would hide our extravagant thoughts amidst rusty spots of labour

if we lived daily facing a great river

we would turn into Li Bai by simply living

I'd like to adapt a song by changing its title

as 'My Home is on the Sandbar in the Heart of a River'

with the next line that goes, 'Here's my beloved so and so'

农家菜馆

菊叶蛋汤、清炒芦蒿、马齿苋烧肉
江虾炒韭菜、凉拌马兰头
读一张菜单像是在读田野的家谱

宽大的餐桌像沙场，摆在篱笆围起的露天小院
我们要把江心洲的四季
品尝、咀嚼，吞咽，并且消化

月亮升起来
给每个菜里加了一点甜味

六只红灯笼悬挂在屋门前
里面裹着晕黄的寂静
屋檐下的斗笠用庄稼的筋骨编成
它有一个像它的红飘带那样的好心情
还有那些玉米串，看上去多么实心眼啊
老板娘把我们当成太阳来奉承
她的脸是一朵向日葵

月亮升起来

盘子里的盐水鸭头带着淡淡的愁容

它们突然怀念起不远处的池塘

从灵魂深处发出嘎嘎嘎嘎的呼唤

那些虾子随时准备消褪红色，游回江里

油汪汪的霉干马齿苋很想还原叶绿素，种回山坡和洼地去

重新发芽

坐在我面前的男人在喝啤酒

我对他的爱最好是先别说出来

我的目光越过他的肩头，越过篱笆

到了对面的果园

而我的心走得更远

它早就到了两公里外的江面，乘上了一艘远洋货轮

月亮升起来了

又大又圆

就当免费上来的一盘果酱吧

A Rural Restaurant

chrysanthemum leaf egg soup, stir-fried Artemisia selengensis, pork stewed
    with horse-tooth pussley
leek stir-fried with river shrimps and Indian Kalimeris herb dressed cold
reading the menu felt like reading the genealogy of a field

the table, vast like a battlefield, was set up in a small open courtyard,
    fenced with a hedge
where we'd like to taste, chew, swallow and digest
the four seasons of the sandbar in the heart of a river

the moon was rising
sweetening up each and every dish

six red lanterns, hanging in front of the door
had the fuzzy yellow quietness wrapped inside them
a bamboo hat, under the eaves, and plaited with the sinews of the crop
had a good feeling about itself like its own red ribbon
and those strings of corn looked so one-track minded
the boss lady flattered us, treating us like the sun
her face a sunflower

the moon was rising

the heads of the salted duck in the plate looked slightly sad

as they suddenly started missing the pond nearby

sending forth quack-quack calls from the depths of their souls

the shrimps, ready to shed their redness, would love to swim back to the
river

while the oily dry horse-tooth pussley would like to recover its chlorophyll
and get planted back on the hill slope or low-lying land

to bud again

the man sitting in front of me was drinking beer

I'd better not voice my love of him

and I looked across his shoulder, across the hedge

to reach the orchard opposite us

my heart going even further

as it had gone on board an ocean liner, on the river, two kilometres away

the moon had risen

huge and round

let's take it for a plate of jam

那些货轮

我们说的是那些从上游和中游来的货轮
当岛上喜欢早睡的人把灯光都熄了
唯有我们的房屋彻夜长明
它们会不会把这临江的窗口误当成灯塔
带着万吨的希望不顾一切地朝这边开过来
把江堤撞毁?

我们说的是那些从居所前面驶过的货轮
它们装着木头、钢材或粮食缓缓前行
在我们半掩的窗前埋下伏笔
在那略显压抑的笛声里
有着放之四海而皆准的音节
可以听出过剩的力比多

那些吃苦耐劳的货轮,那些巨人
用载重准确地测出了一条江的肺活量
用笛音的粗细长短测出你这个土著的血压
以及我这个异乡人的心率
在终将到达航道尽头时
它们一定会感到孤独

我们说的是那些货轮

我们坐在黄昏的江堤上说的是那些货轮

夕阳把江水浸染得多么悲壮

忽然我在某个船尾的货物标识的产地上

认出了遥远的北方，我的家乡

The Cargo Ships

we are talking about the cargo ships from the upstream or midstream

when early sleepers on the island turn off the lights

ours is the only house that remains lit all night

would the ships mistake this window facing the river as a lighthouse

and rush this way, recklessly, with its ten-thousand tons of hope

breaking the embankment?

we are talking about the cargo ships that go past our residence

with timber, steel or foodstuff

foreshadowing themselves before our window that is ajar

in the slightly suppressed siren

there are syllables that are universally correct

from which one could detect the surplus libido

those hard-working cargo ships, the giants

have accurately measured the lung capacity of a river, with their loads

and tested the blood pressure of you, an aboriginal, and the heart rates of

me, an alien, with the size of its siren

they'd feel lonely

when they reach the end of the line

we are talking about the cargo ships

and while we are sitting on the dusky embankment we are talking about
    them

the setting sun has dyed the waters in such solemnity

when, all of a sudden, I recognised my hometown in the far north

from the location labeled on the cargo at the stem of a ship

水杉啊水杉

我爱你们，这些种在长长道路两旁的水杉
我第一眼望过去的时候，就爱上了你们

我爱你们的高，你们的瘦，你们的直
你们的彬彬有礼，你们眉清目秀的好年龄
你们的愁肠和多情的身子骨
还有像烟一样轻灵薄透的神情

潮湿的大地通过你们
进行深呼吸，并与云彩联络着感情
身上的细长枝叶能排列出无数象形文字
你们这些舞文弄墨的才子啊
在江南妩媚的天空下一路风光，浪得虚名

你们不知道，那路旁开蓝色小花的鸭趾草
也为你们害了相思病
我心口的一颗痣正因激动而颜色加深

为你们，我远离了我的杨树的故乡
是的，我承认，我曾经深深地爱过白杨

它们在郊外一排一排地站立，像是豪言壮语
每棵树都有沙沙作响的青春
苦命的麻雀栖落在它们的肩上

在爱过白杨之后，现在我竟又开始爱上了水杉
并心甘情愿成为这里的囚犯
我要沿着这条两旁长满水杉的乡间道路一直走下去
能走多远就走多远

Dawn Redwoods, Oh, Dawn Redwoods

I love you, the dawn redwoods lining the road

in the first glance I took at you, I fell in love

I love your height, your thinness, your straightness

your good manners and your good age of delicate features

your sad hearts and amorous bones

as well as your transparently light looks

the moistened land takes deep breaths

through you and emotionally communicates with the clouds

your branches, long and thin, can form lines of countless hieroglyphs

oh, your talents, dancing in ink

are so vainglorious, enjoying yourselves so much, under the pretty skies of

    River South

that you are hardly aware of the duck-foot grass, in blue bloom, by the

    roadside

is also lovesick of you

while the mole at the mouth of my heart is deepening in colour

because of you, I've left my hometown of poplar trees

yes, I admit, I've deeply loved the white poplars

that stood row after row on the outskirts, like grandiloquences each with a soughing youth

on its shoulders perched the sparrows

having loved the white poplars, I now have begun loving the dawn

    redwoods

willing to become a prisoner of here

where I've liked to walk, keep walking, along the country road, lined with

    it

as far as I can get

菜地

我和你走进菜地
夹道欢迎的是高个子的菊花叶和芹菜
蕃茄唱起红红的颂歌
蚕豆花的黑眼睛明眸善睐
萝卜举着喜庆的缨子，辣椒张灯结彩

这是一个好日子
繁荣和丰收在脸上一望无边
要不要，就在今天就在这菜地里成亲？
我们踩在松软的田埂上，风吹过来
把我这个想法翻译成你的扬州话

我们走到了菜地中央
如果把歇脚处的一簇苜蓿看成老家
跨着那些匍匐的南瓜秧子过去
一直向前，走到那大片油菜花的尽头，就算到了天涯
一堆掰下来的莴苣叶正在溪边快乐地腐烂
多像这个就要过去的春天

我和你一起走在菜地

我围绕着你走，时前时后，时左时右

我知道，我这只北方的青虫

已经一头栽进了你这棵南方的菜心里

The Vegetable Plot

you and I were walking into the vegetable plot

when we were welcomed by the tall chrysanthemum leaves and celery

the tomatoes singing red eulogies

the black eyes of broad bean flowers being great spotters

the turnips holding up the celebratory tassels and the chilies, like decorated
    lanterns

this was a good day

prosperity and harvest endless on its face

shall we have our wedding here today?

we trod the soft ridges as the wind came blowing

turning my thought into your Yangzhou dialect

we had now reached the middle of the plot

if, regarding the cluster of alfalfa where we rested as our native home

we went forward across the pumpkin seedlings lying around

till we reached the end of the expansive canola flowers, treating that as the
    end of the world

where a stack of stripped leaves of the lettuces lay happily rotting
    away

looking so much like this passing spring

you and I were walking in the vegetable plot

I, encircling you, forward-backward, and right-left

as I knew that this green worm that was me

had fallen headlong into the heart of that southern vegetable that was you

傍晚

风从南面吹来
吹过江堤，吹过麻雀翅膀，吹过村庄的衣裳
当它吹过我和你的头顶时
不知不觉换成了最温柔的口气

大半个太阳脑袋被按入水杉林
那在最后夕光里弯向菜地的身躯
像是朝大地做着晚祷
那单腿站立的稻草人
在渐暗的光线里突然感到举目无亲
当最后一辆人力车吆喝着驶过了路面
整整一天的尘埃全部落定

我听见江水在不远处轻轻叹息
蜗牛粘在潮湿的屋顶
脚下的野菊在暮色里摇晃出沙沙声
一只蜥蜴在石头上留下了褐色的卑微的姓氏

这个傍晚多么轻，多么让人心疼
从什么时候起，你已轻轻揽起了我的腰

就像搂着一捆刚刚割下来的草
哦我是你臂弯里的一捆青草
是江心洲的草，是灯心草

In the Evening

when the wind came blowing from the south
across the embankment, the wings of the sparrows and the clothes of the
    village
and when it came blowing over your head and mine
it changed into a most tender breath, without realising what it's doing

the best part of the sun's head pressed into the dawn redwood forest
and the person, bent over his vegetable plot in the last evening glow
looked like he was praying over the land
the scarecrow, standing on one leg
had a sudden feeling in the darkening light that he had no kin to turn to
and when the last rickshaw ran across the road with a yell
the day's dust had all come to settle

I could hear the river sighing not far off
a snail getting stuck on the wet roof
wild chrysanthemum at my foot shaking with a soughing sound at dusk
and a lizard leaving its humble brown name on a stone

this evening was so light, and so cherished
I knew not when your arm, lightly, encircled my waist
like a bundle of grass, freshly cut

oh, I am a bundle of green grass in your arms

grass on the sandbar in the heart of the river, grass in the heart of a lamp

女儿

我要把女儿生在江心洲
生在一棵紫楝树下，一簇野菊花旁
我用乳汁喂养她，大江在身边日夜奔流

她是我的美丽的独生女
4/4拍的啼哭惊飞白鹭
她的姓氏里有三点水做偏旁
名字是这岛上的某种植物，笔划里有草字头
我喊她的时候，露珠闪烁，风吹草动
大江在身边日夜奔流

春天大片油菜花会当成她的布匹
秋天的果园就是她的首饰店
夏天在她的头发上留下缕缕草香
冬天里阳光缠绕着她的细腰，那是世界尽头
她以亚热带的天空为信仰一天一天长大
大江在身边日夜奔流

愿她长大以后不要学我
把一生荒废在一个叫做诗歌的菜园

使幸福渺茫得成为一只萤火虫

要像向日葵那样好好学习，像节节草那样天天向上

祝她前程远大，就像这大江日夜奔流

哦，我的肚子在江南的天空下日渐隆起

变成受人尊敬的样子

我在荆钗布裙下裹着山河，忘记前半生的苦

和后半生的愁

一条大江啊是知音，在身边日日夜夜地向着大海奔流

My Daughter

I would love to give birth to my daughter on the sandbar in the heart of the
    river
underneath a purple china tree, near a cluster of wild chrysanthemums
where I'd breastfeed her, next to the great river running day and night

she would be my beautiful only daughter
scaring off the white egrets with her cries at 4/4 tempo
she would have a surname with three drops of water for a radical
and her given name would be a plant on this island, with a grass radical in
    its strokes
if I called her by her name, dews would twinkle and wind would move the
    grass
and the river would be running by her side, day and night

spreads of canola flowers in spring would be her cloth
the orchard in autumn, her jewelry shop
the summer would leave crisps of grass fragrance in her hair
while, in winter, the sun would encircle her thin waist, the end of the
    world
she would grow up, with her faith being the subtropical skies
and the river would be running by her side, day and night

I wish she would not learn from me

by wasting her whole life in a vegetable garden called poetry

and rendering happiness as rare as a firefly

instead, she ought to learn from the sunflowers and grow up daily, like the
  step-step grass

and I hope she has a great career ahead of her, like this river, running day
  and night

oh, my baby bump was getting bigger every day, under the skies of River
  South

in a shape that commanded respect

and, wrapping the mountains and rivers beneath my cloth skirt, I forget

the bitterness of the first half of my life

and the sadness of my second half

the river being my alter-ego, running by my side towards the sea, day and
  night

外省的爱情

我是爱你的，请不要怀疑。
这外省的爱情摇摇晃晃地走在旅途上
扛着太多的行李。
我来自一个出圣人的省份
我是它的逆女
活了三十年，像找寻首都一样
找到江心洲
像找寻真理一样找到了你。
我爱你，请不要怀疑。
还记不记得，去年我带着一大摞煎饼去看你
那后来成为我们俩两天两夜的口粮
在祖国辽阔的大地上
我是一只驮着希望的小蚂蚁
对命运感激的泪水流了上千里。
我是爱你的，我隔着中国最长的河爱你
隔着中国最雄伟的山爱你。
在我的心里，我以我家附近那条生长法桐的东西马路为界
　　线

把包括我的住宅在内的以南地区
统统划归了你所在的那个南面邻省
让我的八里洼与你的江心洲结成亲戚。
我是爱你的，请不要怀疑。

Love in the Provinces

I am in love with you. Please don't doubt it.

this love in the provinces is wobbly on its journey

carrying too much luggage.

a rebel

I come from a province of saints

having lived thirty years, I've found you

like I've found the truth

having found the sandbar in the heart of the river, like a capital.

I love you; please don't doubt it.

remember I went to see you last year with a big pile of pancakes

that ended up becoming our food for two days and nights

on the vast land of motherland

I am an ant, carrying hope on its back

my tears, appreciative of Fate, running thousands of kilometres

but I am in love with you, loving you from the other side of the longest

river in China

and from the other side of the most spectacular mountain in China, too.

in my heart, I regard the East-West street, lined with French plane trees,

near my home, as a boundary

assigning all the area, including my residence, south of the region

to the adjacent province where you are based

allowing my Baliwa to be a relative of your Jiangxinzhou, the sandbar in
    the heart of the river
I am in love with you. Please don't doubt it.

十年

计划中的十年，不长也不短
足以使我结识这个岛上的每一棵树
叫出每一株草的芳名
足以使葡萄园吸干大地里的甜
足以使江水把大堤的石头冲刷得发亮
使枇杷树下的那只小猫成为最老的祖母
使一只蚂蚁从岛的最南头行至最北头
使我从诗人变成农妇
再从农妇变成诗人

啊十年不短也不长
足以使体内的器官经历战争与和平
生命进入秋天
足以使我们像曾经的那样
杳无音讯八年，再相约见面
足以使你穿过层层淤积的黑暗
挖掘出我身上的那个楼兰

Ten Years

the ten years in my plan are neither long nor short
enough for me to be acquainted with every tree on this island
and to be able to call every grass by its scented name
enough for the grape garden to suck dry the sweet from the earth
for the river water to scour the stones of the embankment till they shine
for the small cat under the loquat tree to become the oldest grandma
for an ant to travel from the southernmost end of the island to its
      northernmost
and for me to turn into a peasant woman, and back into a poet

ah, ten years are neither short nor long
enough for my internal organs to experience war and peace
till my life enters into the autumn
enough for us to be what it was like before
gone missing for eight years before we met again, by appointment
and enough for you to go through layers of accumulated darkness
to dig up the Loulan,[1] from within me

---

[1] Translator's note—a country in ancient China that disappeared about 1600 years ago.

我一个人生活

我一个人生活
上顿白菜炒豆腐，下顿豆腐炒白菜
外加一小碗米饭。
这些东西的能量全都用来
打长途，跑火车，和你吵架，与你相爱
我吃着泰山下的粮食，黄河边的菜
心思却在秦岭淮河以南。
我的消化系统竟这样辽阔
差不多纵横半个祖国
胃是丘陵隆起，肠道是江河蜿蜒。
我就这样一个人生活着
眼睛闪亮，头发凌乱
一根电话线和一条铁路线做了动脉血管。
我就这样孜孜不倦地生活着
爱北方也爱南方，还爱我的破衣烂衫
一年到头，从早到晚。

I Live Alone

I live my life alone

with bok choy, stir-fried with tofu, for last meal, and tofu, stir-fried with
    bok choy for next

plus a small bowl of rice

all of its energy is used

making long-distance phone calls, travelling by train, arguing with you and
    loving you

I eat the food at the foot of Mount Tai and the vegetables on the Yellow
    River

while my mind is occupied with things south of the Qinling Mountains
    and the Huai River

my digestive system so vast

it covers almost half of the motherland

my stomach bulging like a hill and my intestines meandering like a river

thus I live alone

my eyes shining, my hair messy

a telephone line and a railway line forming the artery vessels

I thus live alone

loving the North as much as I love the South, and I also love my tattered
    clothes

all the year round, from morning till night

两只蝴蝶

一只黄蝴蝶和一只白蝴蝶
一个蝴蝶公子一个蝴蝶小姐
从一朵喇叭花花心的公寓里飞出
飞过菜地，飞过荷塘，飞过芦苇丛
飞过两旁长着蚕豆的土路
来到了江堤上

这是两只江苏的蝴蝶
它们有秦淮风韵，有才子才女之相
属于这江心洲上的小资
它们身穿苏绣的丝绸薄衫
用吴侬软语说着海誓山盟
甚至还唱了一段昆曲，吟了一首《蝶恋花》
它们自认为一个是李香君一个是候方域
而我山东老家的蝴蝶们，要比它们敦厚些本分些
那里的蝴蝶不会唱戏做诗，却能背诵《论语》

两只蝴蝶在我们身旁叽叽哝哝
我请求你这个本地人，将它们的语言翻译成普通话
因为我听来听去，似乎只听懂了那么一句

我听见那只白蝴蝶对那只黄蝴蝶说

"瞧这个北方女人，多么土气啊！"

Two Butterflies

a yellow butterfly and a white one

a butterfly gentleman and a butterfly miss

are flying out of an apartment in the heart of a morning glory

across a vegetable plot, a lotus pond, a cluster of rushes

and an earthen road, lined with the growing broad beans

till they arrive at the river bank

these are the two butterflies from Jiangsu

they have the wind rhythm of the Qinhuai River, and the facial features of

    a man and a woman, both talented

petty bourgeois who belong to this sandbar in the heart of the river

they wear thin silk garments of Su embroidery

exchanging solemn vows in the soft Wu dialect

so much so that one sings a number of Kun opera and the other, 'A

    Butterfly in Love with a Flower'

the female thinks of herself as Li Xiangjun and the male, as Hou Fangyu[2]

and the butterflies in my hometown are more dutiful than them

who, unable to sing or write poetry, can recite *The Analects*

---

[2] Translator's note—both Li Xiangjun and Hou Fangyu are characters from a play, titled, 'A Peach-flower Fan', by Kong Shangren, published in 1699, Li being a prostitute, then a concubine of Hou, a man of letters.

the two butterflies are whispering around us

can I ask you, a local, to turn their language into Mandarin

because I, after much listening to it, manage to understand only this

from what the white butterfly said to the yellow:

'look, how earthen this Northern woman is!'

过江

这条大江是我们的边境线

两岸草木信誓旦旦，怀着从唐古拉山到东海的巨大耐心

当火车铿锵着驶过江上铁桥

我开足马力的心开始变得缓慢

与衣裳一起飞扬的风已越过七个城市的孤独

现在终于爱上了这宽阔的江面

和那些船只的飘飘衣袂

我在6号车厢倚窗而坐

车头已经到了江南，车尾还在江北

这列曾穿透长城内外的火车此刻又横跨大江南北

它的经历这样广袤

随身携带的圣旨渐变为丝竹之声

翻山越岭的信念成为一块抖动的印花披巾

我在手机短信里告诉你"我正在过江"

我不是百万雄师，我只是由一个人组成的部队

全部装备是一小罐槐花蜜

它来自北方晴朗的五月

带着一个小镇的寂静和体温

Crossing the River

this big river is our borderline

trees and grasses on either of its banks vowing in all sincerity, with an

 enormous patience that stretches from the T'ang-ku-la Mountains to

 the East China Sea

when the train runs across the iron bridge on the river

my heart, full of steam, is beginning to slow down

and the wind, flying with my clothes, has crossed the solitude of seven

 cities

and finally fallen in love with this vastness of the river

and the floating sleeves of those boats

I sit by the window in No. 6 compartment

the head of my train has arrived in River South although its tail remains in

 River North

a train that has travelled through the Great Wall, within and without, is

 now crossing the Yangtze, from north to south

its experience so boundless

that the edict it carries is now turning into the silk and bamboo music

and the belief in climbing the mountains, now a printed scarf

in a text I sent you by mobile phone I said to you, 'I'm crossing the river'

not one of a million bold warriors, I am a one-woman troop

armed with a tiny pot of acacia honey

from a fine May in the North

carrying the quietness and bodily warmth of a small town

忆扬州

来一盘煮干丝，两个狮子头，一壶碧螺春
如果没有琼花露，那就上两瓶茉莉花牌啤酒吧
我们喝了一杯又一杯
这是我和你的扬州

何必腰缠十万贯只须揣百元钞票，何须骑鹤只须乘高速大
　宇
就有勇气下扬州

这是在梦中，有你的梦中，十年一觉的梦中
窗外千年的绿水悠悠
积压发霉的诗词生成砖缝中的苔痕
历经无数个烟花三月的是那些阁那些寺那些亭
我说，我想把弹琴当功课，把栽花当种田
而你呢，就去做一个文章太守

当微醉之后摇晃着走在石板路上
我相信这个夜晚的明月是从杜牧诗中
复制并粘贴到天上去的
哦请告诉我，告诉我哪是黛玉离家北上的码头

我们这样沿着运河走，在到达宾馆之前
会不会遇上南巡并且微服的乾隆

Remembering Yangzhou

bring us a plate of boiled dry bean curd slices, two lion-head meatballs, and
    a pot of Biluo Spring tea
if there is no Jade Flower Dew, then bring us two bottles of Jasmine Flower
    Beer
we've downed one glass after another
and this is my Yangzhou and yours

no need to be cashed-up as a few 100-yuan notes would be enough nor any
    need to ride a crane but just hop onto a high-speed Daewoo
with enough courage to go downstream to Yangzhou

this is in a dream, a dream with you in it, a dream one takes ten years to
    wake up from
in which there are thousand-year-long green waters outside the window
and moldy poems and *ci* have turned into traces of moss between the bricks
what have experienced endless Marches of smoky flowers are those temples
    and pagodas and pavilions
and I said, I'd like to strum a lute like having classes and to plant flowers
    like farming a field
and, as for you, you can go and be a governor of literary articles

when I walk, slightly tipsy, on the flagstone road
I believe that the night's moon is from a Du Mu poem

copied and pasted on the sky

oh, please tell me where the port is where Daiyu left her home

and if we may run into Emperor Qianlong, travelling incognito on his tour

before we arrive at our hotel walking along the Great Canal

鱼塘

我相信那些鱼都睡着了，所以不见踪影
红鲤该有年画上的模样，这方水塘是金色屋子
用来藏娇。
破烂的鱼网扔在地上，供麻雀结绳记事。
紧靠岸边的，仿佛是伏羲或神农留下来的
一只失去双橹的木船。
藻类絮絮叨叨，话题挤向水塘四个边缘。
那些逐水而居的灌木临帖着北风
把自己的姓和名写下来
用勇气顶住了江南冬天的微寒。
当我和你走过，我说，要小心，要小心
这岸边的泥土很软，跟春天时候一样
那么容易塌陷！

The Fishpond

I believe those fish have gone to sleep, which is why there's not a trace
the red carp look like those on a New-Year painting, and this square of a
      pond is a gold house
for hiding beautiful things in
where a rotten fishing net, thrown on the ground, is meant for the sparrows
      to keep records by tying the knots
and, close to the riverbank, is a wooden boat without the oars
looking as if it had been left there by Fu Xi or Shen Nong.
the algae are babbling, about a subject that is squeezed to the four corners
      of the pond
and the bushes that live by the waterside are practicing calligraphy against
      the northern wind
writing down their own surnames and given names
pitted against the slight cold of River South with courage.
when you and I walked by, I said: Be careful, be careful
as the soil by the waterside is soft, like in spring
so easy to collapse!

今当永诀

告诉桃花，不要开了
我没有绯红的心情与它交相辉映
让蜜蜂歇息，不要嗡嗡嗡地忙着说媒
请土壤里的蚯蚓停止做白日梦吧
还有，请云层使劲忍住，别将雨水滴落
让田畴、山坡和道路都保持灰色，安于清贫

通知大地不要将春天拼写出来
声母丢弃韵母，平声背叛仄声，形旁和声旁就此分别
那些笔画，点横竖撇捺弯勾，全都忘记了诺言
爱已成死灰永不复燃，我和那个人也成为彼此的旧病
我在北，他在南，一条长江从此真的做了天堑

如果可能，我还想把两个城市之间的铁轨拆除
把航班去消，把高速公路毁掉，把通讯电缆掐断
网络联接最好也出现故障
因为所有这一切都没有用处了——
我和那个人虽然都还活着，却仿佛已阴阳相隔！

Time to Part for Good

tell the peach flowers not to open any more

I'm not in a pink mood to match their splendour

let the bees take a rest from buzzing about dating

and get the earthworms in the soil to stop daydreaming

and also get the clouds to hold from raining

so that the fields, the slopes and the roads keep grey, at ease with poverty

let the land not spell out the word 'chuntian' (spring)

when the initial consonants abandon the vowels, the level tones rebel

      against the falling tones and all the strokes forget their promises

when love turns into dead ashes, with that person and I having become

      each other's old illness

I in the North and he in the South, the Yangtze now really a sky chasm

if possible at all, I'd like to remove the railway lines between the two cities

to cancel the flights, to destroy the highway and to cut the communications

      cables

better still, to cause the internet connections to malfunction

because nothing of this will be of any use any more—

I and that person, although still alive, are separated by yin and yang, it

      seems!

在临安

在临安，我食竹笋咸肉、莼菜汤和小黄鱼
还有青团，用艾草汁揉和糯米面又裹了豆沙馅的
品着从围墙外的山上采回的龙井
我愿为这些美味丢职弃爵
是的，我几乎忘了随身携带的悲伤，忘了你

在临安，我认识了木荷、香樟树、杪椤和岩柏
这些植物用全身心的淡淡苦香抚慰我
从早晨到黄昏雨丝都飘在半空
走遍座座小山，衣袖已被染绿
我真的就要把你忘记

我见到多年未见的老友
红砖小楼下的水洼传来青蛙的咏叹调
凉台上有安居乐业的盆花
门厅里摆着懂中庸之道的躺椅
那些餐具在厨房里保持着好脾气
是的，我来到临安，就是为了不再把你想起

我枕着山睡去，傍着云醒来

一阵小风在测量我的身材

这是临安，是李白和苏东坡来过的临安

唉，为了忘记你，我一口气跑出来两千三百里

At Lin'an

at Lin'an, I ate salty pork, stir-fried with bamboo shoots, soup of water
     shield and small yellow fish
and there were also green dumplings, made of sticky rice powder, mixed
     with the liquid of Artemisia argyi, with red bean paste
as I tasted the Dragon Well tea, its leaves gathered from the hill outside the
     wall
I'd love to give up everything for this
yes, I've almost forgotten the sadness I've brought with me, I've forgotten
     you

at Lin'an, I got to know about superba, camphora, spinulose tree ferns and
     rock cypresses
all these plants comfort me with their whole-hearted light bitter fragrance
from morning till dusk, a fine drizzle was drifting in the air
as I walked from hill to hill, my clothes and sleeves dyed green
I really was at the point of forgetting you

I met old friends I had not met for years
an aria of frogs came from the puddles outside the red-brick buildings
where, on the balconies, there were potted plants, settled and happy
and there was a deck chair in the hallway, one that was aware of the golden
     mean

the utensils in the kitchen were sweet-tempered

yes, I came to Lin'an in order to forget you

I fell asleep on the pillow of the mountain and I woke up leaning against a
     cloud

a breeze was taking my body measurements

this is Lin'an, that once saw the arrival of Li Bai and Eastern Slope Su

well, in order to forget you, I'd covered two thousand and three hundred *li*
     in one breath

在增城吃荔枝有感

荔枝相当于水果中的贵妇
就像杨梅和樱桃
是水果中的小姐和丫环

它被一个皇帝用来讨好
他的某个妃子
在没有高速公路和波音飞机的时代
这是一个劳民伤财的故事
是一个生活奢侈豪华的故事
是红颜祸水的证据
被看成亡国的原因之一
是的，我们不妨说，是荔枝颠覆了
中国历史上最强盛的朝代
我们也可以说，这就是爱情呢
要以一个王朝的毁灭为代价

其实所有的爱情都是昂贵的
都像荔枝一样容易腐烂，朝不保夕
为了保鲜，必须日夜兼程

使人筋疲力尽
并且累死许多匹马

这是爱情故事中惟一与吃有关的
在我看来，这首先是一个吃的故事
其次才是爱情故事
它使我想起在我的学生时代
差点儿因为一个男生送的一袋巧克力
而以身相许

如今我快到了杨贵妃缢死马嵬坡的年龄
我没心没肺地活着
乘飞机跑出4000里来到广东增城
自己买荔枝给自己吃
从"桂味"、"糯米糍"、"水晶球"，一直到"挂绿"
如果按古代的成本计算
我差不多吃掉了半个大唐江山
如今，谁也不是我的唐玄宗
我也只是我自己的杨贵妃
我走到哪里，哪里就是长安

Thoughts on Eating Lychees in Zengcheng

a lychee is equivalent to a lady amongst fruits
the same way a waxberry and a cherry
are, respectively, a maid and a servant girl among the same

once there was an emperor who used her
to please one of his imperial concubines
a story of wasteful expenses
in an age of no freeways or Boeing aircrafts
a story, too, of luxurious extravagances
evidence of whorishly disastrous pink features
that's regarded as one of the leading causes for the fall of a nation
yes, we might even say that it is the lychee that subverted
the most powerful dynasty in the history of China
and we might also say that, well, this is love
that comes at the price of the demise of a kingdom

in fact, all love is precious
easy to rot, fresh in the morning, gone by the evening
and, to keep it fresh, one has to run day and night
till one is exhausted
and many a horse dies

that is one of the only love stories related to eating

and, in my view, it is a story of eating

before it is a story of love

as it reminds me of myself in my school days

when I was almost head over heels

for a bag of chocolates, a gift from a boy student

now, at nearly the age of Imperial Concubine Yang Guifei when she was

      hanged at Mawei Slope

I live, quite heartless

So much so that I came two thousand kilometres to Zengcheng, Guangzhou

      by plane

just to buy the lychees, to eat for myself

from Laurel Taste, Glutinous Rice, Crystal Ball to Green Hanging

I've eaten half of the mountains and rivers of the Great Tang Dynasty

if calculated at the ancient cost

but, now, no one is my Emperor Xuanzong of Tang

and I am my own Yang Guifei

wherever I go, there Chang'an is

横贯公路

从东往西，往西，沿着横贯公路走
一辆红色吉普穿过美利坚合众国
远远铺展开来，这平原，这牧场，这天空，这命运
我把前半生抛在了后头

沿着横贯公路走，经过小镇和乡村的时候
看见它们静立花丛，并把一本《圣经》摆放在胸口
牛群担负着一个国家的肠胃
湖里有野鸭，树间有麋鹿，田里种着马铃薯、玉米和大豆

沿着横贯公路走啊，沿着横贯公路走
用四个轮子量出一个大陆，这是最长最热烈的摇滚
我装了满满一脑袋仓颉造的古老汉字
在别人的祖国我想唱一曲《乌苏里江》，一展歌喉

沿着横贯公路走啊沿着横贯公路走，东和西永无尽头
地平线是信仰，千里万里无遮无挡
白云在蓝蓝的天上一动不动，踩一下油门就可以追上
啊，只需踩一下油门，我就能到天上
夕阳正朝整个大陆挥舞着宽大的衣袖

沿着横贯公路走啊，沿着横贯公路走

过了密苏里大桥，就从爱荷华到了内布拉斯加州

在奥马哈城外，一场电闪雷鸣的暴雨在致欢迎辞

就这样沿着横贯公路走，按1：8计算，"哪里用美元买的东

西最多"

哪里就是家门口

Highway Across the Country

from the east to the west, further west, along the highway

a red jeep is crossing the United States of America

that spreads itself out in the distance, with this prairie, this ranch, this sky

    and this fate

I have left the first half of my life behind me

along this highway, when I go through small towns or villages

I see them quiet among the flowers, with a Bible on their chests

the cattle bearing the stomach and intestines of a nation

while there are wild ducks in the lakes, deer in the woods, potatoes, maize

    and soybeans in the fields

oh, I travel along this highway, this highway

measuring a continent with my four wheels, in the longest and hottest rock

    and roll

my head filled with the ancient Chinese characters, created by Cang Jie

and, even if this is someone else's country, I'd love to sing the song, 'The

    Ussuri', to show off my voice

going along this highway, this highway, endlessly from east to west

the horizon being a faith and the length, unstoppable

white clouds motionless in the blue skies that I can overtake them if I slam

    my foot on the gas

and indeed I can reach the sky if I slam it

where the setting sun is waving its broad sleeves to the whole continent

going along the highway, along the highway

arriving in Nebraska from Iowa once over the Missouri River Bridge

and, outside Omaha, a thunderous rainstorm is making a welcome speech

and if one keeps going along the highway, home is wherever

'one could buy most things' at the exchange rate of 1 USD to 8 RMB

露营

今夜，我的床是整个一张北美大陆
南达科他州平原是一面方形床单
一本世界地图册当了枕头
这里只有天空，只有天空中的云
与我的祖国相连

密苏里河从身旁缓缓流过
我体内有长江黄河的节拍与它呼应
不远处的廊桥是不是曾在书中读到的那一座
附近的篝火发出噼噼叭叭的响声，可否把乡愁朗诵
当祖国从太平洋彼岸醒来，我正准备入睡
此刻我有着中英文对照的心情

在梦里我会把帐篷上空的满天星斗
由拼音文字译成象形文字
把遍地蔓延的惠特曼的草叶读成李白的苍苔和蒲柳
把狄金森的苜蓿或石楠读成李清照的海棠
从身旁跑过的松鼠会像衔走松果那样
衔走我的片言只语

当东边天色微明，那是太阳从我祖国的方向升起
一群火鸡飞过橡树林
用流利的英语啼叫把我吵醒

Camping

tonight, my bed is the whole North-American continent

the South Dakota Prairie is a square bed-sheet

a world atlas serves as my pillow

here, there are only the skies, and only the clouds in the skies

are connected to my motherland

the Missouri River sluggishly flows away by my side

the Yangtze River and the Yellow River inside me are echoing with it in
  rhythm

I wonder if the bridge nearby is one of the ones of Madison County in a
  book I read

the bonfire, not far off, is crackling, by which one can read aloud one's
  nostalgia

when my motherland wakes up on the other side of the Pacific, I am about
  to sleep

and right now I am in a bilingual mood

in my dream I shall translate a skyful of stars over my tent

from the phonetic into the pictographic

I'll read the sprawling Whitmanesque leaves of grass into Li Bai's green
  moss and big catkin willow

or Dickinson's alfalfa or moor besom into Li Qingzhao's begnonia

while the squirrel that is running past me will pick up my words between
    its teeth
the way it does the pinecones

when the sky is faintly light in the east, it'll be the place where the sun
    rises in my motherland
there a group of turkeys flies through the oak forest
waking me up with their fluent English

殖民客栈

鲜花攻陷了有圆柱的门廊
我入住进一国的史书，是扉页和前言

感谢侍者除了预备房间
还安排了一场小雨
雨点落入黄昏，落在1716年陡峭的灰屋顶上
烟囱还是那么热爱天空

存放过武器的厅堂，如今是前台
柠檬冰水和苹果交换着免费的酸与甜
曾救治民兵的诊疗室
萨克斯正吹出自由，大约是龙虾和生蚝奏鸣曲
烤玉米面包散发出新英格兰的清香

我的房间在走廊迷宫的终端
壁炉内三百年前的木柴尚有余温
胡桃木家具上的纹饰是另一时代的缩略语
已经疲于漫长的存在
而wifi，比高铁还快

传说中闹鬼的房间就在头顶
上百年前的幽灵偶尔也会在楼梯徘徊
遇见鬼魂的可能性
想必也被算进了房费，以信用卡支付

拉开窗帘，望见纪念碑，上面镌刻那一年
全地球都听得见的快乐的枪声

The Colonial Inn

the flowers had captured the portico with columns
as I checked into the history book of a nation, its title page and preface

thankful to the bellboy for reserving my room
on top of organising a light rain
whose raindrops were falling into the dusk, on the steep grey roof of 1716
where the chimney was still in such a passionate love of the sky

the hall, where weapons used to be stored, was now the front desk
on which the ice lemonade and apples exchanged sour and sweet for free
in the clinic where the militia once received medical treatment
a saxophone was playing freedom, possibly a sonata of lobsters and raw
      oysters
and the toasted corn bread was smelling of New England

my room was at the end of a maze of corridors
in the fireplace, the firewood three hundred years ago was still warm
the emblazonry on the walnut furniture, an abbreviation of another time
was tired of its long existence
while the wi-fi was faster than the high-speed rail

the haunted room was right above my head

ghosts more than a hundred years ago might still pace to and fro on the

    stairs

so that the possibility of running into them

might have been part of the expenses, paid with a credit card

when I pulled the curtain open, I saw the monument, with the inscribed

    date of the year

in which the happy gunshot could be heard across the world

路过安徒生家门口

亲爱的安徒生，此刻我正路过
你的卡通的故乡
你的家门口——

鞋匠和洗衣妇的儿子
生在棺材板改装的床上，所以天生忧郁
14岁携13克朗远走他乡
从此，稿笺被欧洲的雨雾洇湿
以驿车车轮的节奏
写下满纸寂寞

再苦难的人生也可以过成童话
旅行即梦游，礼帽、手杖、雨伞和皮箱
是仅有的道具
一挥手，它们就跳舞
在光荣的荆棘路上

亲爱的安徒生，我们相识已久
我看见，机场的鲜花全是小意达的花
安检人员都是坚定的锡兵

那个在我护照上盖章的大鼻子男人
分明是大克劳斯

我从中国来，从有宝塔和戏台的国度来
"在中国，皇帝是一个中国人，
他周围的人也是中国人。"
嗯，这是你写的句子

亲爱的安徒生，我抵达哥本哈根
而美人鱼不在，她出访上海EXPO未归
请允许我模仿伊人之姿
侧身跪坐在机场咖啡厅的椅子上

Passing by the Door to Anderson's Home

dear Anderson, I am, right now, passing by

your cartoon native town

the door to your home—

born on a bed, made of a coffin plank, thus born melancholy

and the son of a shoemaker and a laundry woman

you left home at 14, with only 13 Krone, and went far away

your manuscripts had since been moistened in Europe's rain mist

filled with solitude

in the rhythm of a stagecoach

a life, however miserable, could be turned into a fairytale

a journey was a sleepwalk, with a topper, a walking stick, an umbrella and

     a suitcase

the only props

and, with the wave of a hand, they'd start dancing

on a glorious thorny road

dear Anderson, we have known each other for a long time

as I could see that the flowers in the airport were all Little Ida's

the security people were all the Hardy Tin Soldiers

and the big-nosed man who put a seal on my passport

I come from China, a country of pagodas and stages
'in China, an emperor is a Chinese
and the people around him are also Chinese'
well, that's what you wrote

dear Anderson, when I arrived in Copenhagen
the Mermaid was not here, still not back from the Shanghai Expo
so please let me imitate her pose
by kneeling sidewise on a chair in the airport café

母亲的心脏

她的胸部上方偏左，即当年佩戴领袖像章的那个位置
——那个最革命的位置
开始塌陷了

她的曾经被我吮吸过的左乳房的背面那片区域
——那片最慈爱的区域
开始疼痛

她无数次因我的胡闹而生气并且用力的那片面积
——那片最喜欢说教的面积
开始衰败

她的被我的远行而牢牢揪住的那个地方
——那个仿佛被别针穿插的地方
开始退化了

她那已跳动六十多年，其中已为我跳动了四十年的器官
——那个伟大的器官
此刻正因缺氧而悲伤

Mother's Heart

the place up left to her chest, where she wore the Mao badge in those days
—the most revolutionary place
is beginning to collapse

the region behind her left breast that I had suckled
—the kindest region
is beginning to be in pain

the area where she got upset and exerted herself on countless occasions
        because of my misbehaviour
—the most didactic area
is beginning to decline

the place where she was held fast by my going far away
—the place where it felt like being pinned
is beginning to degenerate

her organ that had been beating over 60 years, including 40 for me
—that great organ
is beginning to feel sad for lack of oxygen

邮箱

我们相隔多远？从网易到新浪那么远
邮件在光纤里穿梭
偶尔携带以回形针固定的包裹
字母上浮，汉字在邮箱底部沉没

我写给你的信，你写给我的信
有时同时跑过孤独的山东半岛
半路相遇，佯装不识
继续朝对方营地奔去

我们在邮箱里绝交过19次
运载过胡萝卜、小红辣椒和蜂蜜
偶尔产生这样的念头：
一起在邮箱里过夜

个别时候，鼠标卡哒一声
信会弹跳，改道去流浪、走亲戚
迷途知返或者走失
我曾经丢失过一车干草

大雪封门，树林沉寂

一种不可知的力量使邮箱连接了穹苍

一封你写的邮件穿过茫茫风雪

支撑起我的夜空，把星星旋拧在幕布上

The Mailbox

how far are we from each other? It's so far from NetEase to Sina

when emails shuttle through optical fibres

occasionally carrying a package, fixed with a paperclip

the letters emerge while the Chinese characters sink to the bottom of the
  inbox

the letters I wrote to you and the ones you wrote to me

sometimes ran, simultaneously, across the lonely Shandong Peninsula

and, when they met on the way, they pretended not to know each other

while keeping running towards the other's camp

we severed our relationship over email 19 times

and have transported carrots, little red chili peppers and honey

with occasional thoughts like this:

can we spend the night together in the inbox?

a one-off case saw the mouse click

when the letter bounced and changed its route, roaming around or visiting
  a relative

returning after realising about its error or going missing

I have thus lost a load of hay

the big snow now barring the door and the woods falling silent

an unknown power caused the mailbox to connect with the firmament

when an email, written by you, went through the wind and snow

holding up my night sky and screwing the stars on the curtain

内布拉斯加城

A

这城如此寂静，正好适合我的孤单

仿佛不在地球上，仿佛人类尚未诞生

仿佛还不曾有过时间

寂静为身体镶上一道银边，为心上足发条

我听得见血在脉管里流淌

看得见影子在地上轻轻摇晃

天空低矮，太阳猛烈，云朵舒卷

当它们自己也无法忍受自己时

黄昏将辽阔得一下子伸延至天边

B

路面是红砖的，楼也是，它们怎么跟我一样

都喜欢穿红方格子纯棉？

教堂尖顶笔直，想把天捅破，想弄清自己

究竟指向生前还是死后

蒲公英也有信仰，个个绒球都有一颗扶摇直上的心

在风的恳求下，一朵紫菀开放了

刚好就在我的脚边

走出不到百米，一棵上年纪的山毛榉又拦住了去路

问我可否愿意在那银灰色光滑树皮上

刻下我的姓名

C

中央街道拱起，弧度约等于我对人生的思考

车子从弧的那边露出半个脸

珠宝店橱窗在烈日下反射自身光芒，几乎失明

相比之下，图书馆还算清凉

在一本本书籍的呼吸里歇着

渐渐爱上自己的博学

使得对面的电影院，无法不感到自惭

而旁边小餐馆的心思像汉堡一样简单

把奶酪、牛肉、火鸡腿和沙拉全都露在外面

使人想到这个国家的确够壮，也够胖

D

这城总喜欢把绿树画上额头

以示国家植树节在此发源

我每周必去的银行就在正面画了一棵

淡蓝色支票照亮贫穷的脸

拿出护照，遂想起家在地球那一边

日历多撕一页，时钟多走一圈

兄弟姊妹都在梦中，母亲正拉开蒙蒙亮的窗帘

而父亲睡在一个盒子里，睡回到地壳，睡回到了史前

E
路口只有我一人在等交通信号
鞋底上沾着三万里之外的土
多么遥远，除了太阳月亮，谁都找不到我
拐往旧货铺，花1美元大钞
买到一只木制奶牛，它木墩墩的憨厚对我是一种安慰
是的我需要安慰，我还需要对它倾诉衷肠
而一只布娃娃的衣裳旧了，等着我去抚慰
她那颗亚麻布的心
最后看中的是一只树脂猫头鹰
它是哲学家，该挂在床头
用以指点人生迷津

F
书店叫书籍门诊，名字怪，空间小，却胸怀全球
我总是在午后到来
把买面包的钱挪用为书款
坐下来，用一杯清咖啡加深着阅读
老板娘对诗歌的热爱使我宾至如归
感到在世界任何角落，仅凭分了行的文字
就能找到亲人

可她哪里知道，一个诗人

每写完一首诗就离死亡更近了一步

G

小小的城有一个大大的郊外

白色水塔在举重，用四肢举起上百吨

塔下面，草地连绵，一排山茱萸在湖边照镜子

枝叶花果都长成字母的模样

而我把它们全读成部首和偏旁

穿过红栌的迷茫，会发现一处老磨坊

一具戴花环的十字架竖在它身旁

正仰望着苍天祈祷

用来喂马的干草卷轴，它们在远处的田间

忽然产生了滚动的念头

更远处，一排大雁为绕过一片黑亮的云彩

决定改变飞行的方向

H

一只离群的松鼠在突来的雨里

爬上电线杆，接着把电线当钢丝走出好远

我孤单，但不比它更孤单

路旁沟里一株丰收的野苹果树

不堪重负，把晃悠悠的果子一只只掉到地上

无人摘无人捡无人瞧见，我怎会比它更孤单？

教堂钟声的回音摇落了鹅掌楸的花瓣

它一定比我更孤单

子夜屋顶上的闪电，落在大平原上的雨滴

总是被黎明驱赶着的河口的雾气

远走四方的火车侧身经过，对这不能停靠的小城表示同情

把汽笛长鸣当呐喊，留在半空中

这些，岂不比我更孤单？

I

在一棵巨大白松的庇护下

我的居所有着钢琴的形状

松果在草地上排列着跳跃的音符

爱伦·坡的黑猫从小说里跑了出来，漫步庭院

它的绿宝石眼睛里一定藏着案情

一群纸制卡通狗在走廊里头顶香肠，吐着舌头

在半明半暗中做着恶作剧

墙上告示："龙卷风已把邻州掀翻，屋顶上报警器高度神经

　　质

随时会发出警报，请大家夺路而逃，往地下室"

而一只棕色蜘蛛全然不管这些，还在窗纱上漫步

它的目的地是我的书桌，是稿纸上的半首诗

是诗里写坏了的那一句

隔壁女画家勇敢地把一块块画布统统涂成全黑，取名《时
　间与生命》

时间就是什么都没有，生命只是漆黑一片

J

我拿两根烤肉的细竹签当了筷子

是的，从筷子到刀叉，从茶到咖啡

需要十五个小时的航程

冰箱里，奶酪和豆腐对峙，披萨和面条冷战

在两种文化的交锋和谈判中

我独独爱着青玉米！

以一个出售酒类的小店为中心

而形成的快乐与激情的圆周，一直扩至我的公寓

扩至我端着哥伦比亚干红独酌的夜半深更

黑头发披散开，我想就在今晚就在这门厅里

争取解放，宣布独立

K

我已打定主意：让血液流成一条宽阔平稳的密苏里河

对生活不反抗也不屈从

蜷伏在地上睡觉，喜欢这朴实的灰白色地毯

没有人与我相爱，也可以度过良宵

这里是北美大陆中央，这里离海很远
可是为什么总感到海潮正在上涨
要漫过窗外洁净的街道？
为什么总是在一觉醒来时，恍恍惚惚
以为这是在山东半岛？

L

大平原和河流的内布拉斯加
玉米田已变成锦缎、毛豆地已变成金库
树林将醉成绯红的内布拉斯加
越过太平洋并驱车六个州的内布拉斯加
请这里所有粗大的枫树都答应：
我走的那天，要低垂下枝条，代我向大地请安
我只剩下了半生，请替我做个决定吧：
是该用来流浪
还是该用来结婚？

M

是否我只活在今天，今天是老天的礼品
可是今天又是哪一天
时间本来没有开始，没有结尾，也没有方向
只是人类的假设
它其实更像一条可以任意来去的隧道

那国已3000年，这国才300年
这国在时间之轴上刚刚走到那国的公元前
于是我说，从那个国来到这个国
就等于从21世纪初返回到了殷商时代
只是，它的标志不是青铜器
而是航天飞机和微软

N

这城的寂静适合我的孤单
它们一起散发出清香
"我在这世上已经太孤单了，但孤单得还不够"
再往前，将从孤单走向孤绝
生命会圆满，会充满喜庆地张灯结彩
而此刻，像居住在地球上最后一幢房子里
夜色从露台上把我的身影抹去
蟋蟀的弹奏使得墙角加大了凹陷
我知道，这一个又一个寂静的日子
将发芽，将吐穗开花，将结果，将会有一个总和
但须在另一国度
——永远是，当然是，而只能是

Nebraska City

A

the city was so quiet it matched my solitude

feeling as if I were not on this earth, as if mankind were not yet born

and as if time had never existed

the quietness fringing my body with silver, winding up my heart tight

I could hear blood streaming in my veins

and I could see shadows lightly shaking on the ground

the sky was low, the sun violent and the clouds massing and scattering

till they could no longer stand themselves

when the dusk extended itself to the end of the sky

B

the surface of the road was redbrick and so was the building. How could

     they be like me

both liking to wear cotton clothes of red checks?

the steeple of the church was straight, intending to poke a hole in the sky,

     and wanting to know whether it would

point lifeward or deathward

even dandelions had faith as each and every bobble contained a heart that

     went straight upward

begged by the wind, an aster flower opened

right at my foot

before I went out for a hundred metres an elderly beech tree stood in my
    way
wondering if I'd like to carve my name down
on its smooth silver-grey bark

C

Central Avenue arched, its curve about equivalent to my thinking about life
the car revealed half of its face on the other side of the curve
the window of a jewelry shop went almost blind, reflecting its own light in
    the scorching sun
by comparison, the library was cool
resting amongst the breathings of the books
falling in love with its own erudition
causing the cinema across the road to feel ashamed of itself
and the restaurant nearby had thoughts as simple as a hamburger
exposing all its cheese, beef, turkey legs and salad
reminding one of this nation's sufficient size and strength

D

the city likes to paint the green trees on its forehead
to show that the National Arbor Day originated here
the bank I go to on a weekly basis has on its front a poor face lit up by a
    blue cheque
as soon as I produce my passport I remember the other side of the earth
where, with one more page to rip off the calendar and the clock to do one
    more round

my brother and sister are still asleep and my mother has just drawn open
    the dim curtain
while my father is sleeping in a box till he returns to the earth's crust, to
    prehistory

E

at the crossroads, I was the only one waiting for the traffic lights
my soles stained with earth from thirty thousand *li* away
so remote that no one could find me except the sun and the moon
I turned to go to a second-hand shop, where I bought a wooden cow
for one American dollar, its woodenness a comfort to me
right, I did need comfort as I needed to tell it of my thoughts
and the clothes of a cloth doll were old, waiting for me to console
her heart made of linen
in the end, I set my sights on a resin owl
a philosopher that ought to hang from the head of a bed
to point the way in one's life

F

the bookshop, called Book Clinic, has a strange name and small space, but
    a bosom that can contain the globe
I always arrive there in the afternoon
to appropriate my bread money for the books
and I sit down, to add to my depth of reading, with a cup of clear coffee
the woman boss's love of poetry makes me feel at home
thinking that one could find a loved one everywhere in the world

on the strength of words written in lines

even though she has no idea that when a poet

finishes a poem she is one step closer to death

G

the small city has a large suburb

where a white water tower is weight-lifting, its limbs holding hundreds of

    tons

and under the tower there are rolling meadows, with a row of dogwoods

looking at themselves in the mirror of a lake

all the branches, flowers and fruit grown in the shape of letters

that I manage to read as Chinese radicals, *bushou* or *pianpang*

through the confusion of red sumacs one can find an old mill

with a cross, wearing a wreath next to it

lifting its head and praying to the sky

the hay bales, fodder for the horses, in the distant fields

had a sudden intention of rolling by themselves

further on, a row of swan geese decided to change the direction

in order to skirt the dark shining cloud

H

a stray squirrel, in the sudden rain

climbed up the telephone pole and walked far on the line, treating it like a

    tightrope

I was lonely, but not more so than him

a wild apple tree, with a bumper crop, in a roadside ditch

dropped its swaying apples one after another, unable to bear its own load

how could I be more lonely than it when there was no one to pick them, to

pick them up or to even look at them?

the echoing of the church bell shook off the petals of the aspen tulip

poplars

which must be more lonely than I

midnight lightning over the roof, raindrops that fall on the prairie

fog at the estuary that is always driven away by dawn

the train that sidles along, going everywhere, that shows its sympathy to

the city

where it can't stop, treating its siren as yells that stop mid-air

aren't these more lonely than I?

I

in the shelter of a huge white pine

my place is shaped like a piano

where pinecones are laid over the lawn like leaping musical notes

and Edgar Allen Poe's black cat runs out of a novel to stroll in the courtyard

its emerald eyes possibly hiding a case in them

a group of paper cartoon dogs is holding sausages over their heads in a

corridor, their tongues sticking out

playing a practical joke in the semi-darkness

there is a notice on the wall: 'The tornado has overthrown the adjacent

state and the roof alarm is highly sensitive

ready to warn any time, for everyone to escape, to the basement'

but a brown spider, completely oblivious of this, was strolling on the
    window-screen

its destination being my desk, the half-poem on the manuscript

and the line that was badly written

next door, a woman artist bravely turned all her canvases black, calling
    them 'Time and Life'

time being nothing left and life, a darkness

J

I took two sharpened bamboo BBQ sticks as chopsticks

yes, it would take fifteen hours to fly

from the chopsticks to knives and forks, and from tea to coffee

in the fridge, cheese were facing off against tofu, pizza and noodles were
    engaging in a cold war

in the contest and negotiation of the two cultures

I loved the green corn alone!

a circle of pleasure and passion, with a wine shop

as its centre, extended itself to my apartment

to the midnight when I was holding a glass of Columbia Cabernet
    Sauvignon, drinking alone

my black hair let down, and I'd like to declare independence

in my fight for liberation, tonight in this hallway

K

I'm determined that I shall let my blood run into a broad and steady
    Missouri River

not rebelling against life nor submitting to it

sleeping curled up on the floor as I like this plain white carpet

spending a beautiful night, without having anyone else to love me

it's the centre of the North American continent here, far from the ocean

but why do I always feel the tide is rising

threatening to flood the clean street outside?

and why do I always feel that I'm somehow

in the Shandong Peninsula when I wake up?

L

in Nebraska of the Great Prairie and rivers

cornfields have turned into brocade and green soybean fields, a treasure
    trove

the tree leaves are about to get so drunk that they'll turn into a crimson
    Nebraska

a Nebraska one has to arrive from across the Pacific and drive through six
    states

please can all the thick maple trees here promise:

on the day when I leave, please lower your branches and pay respects to the
    land for me

making a decision for me on the next half of my life:

should I spend it roaming

or getting married?

M

am I only living today, today, a gift from the heavens

but which day is today

time has no beginnings or endings, no directions, either

all just hypothesis by mankind

it in fact is more like a tunnel one can travel through at will

that country is over 3000 years while this one is a mere 300

this country has just reached that country's B.C. on the axis of time

so, I say, arriving in this country from that country

equals a return to the Shang Dynasty from the early 21st century

except that its symbol is not the bronze ware

but space shuttles and micro-software

N

this city's quietness matches my solitude

together, they send forth a clear fragrance

'I'm so lonely in this world but not lonely enough'[3]

if I walk further, I'll move from loneliness to a solitary desolation

when life will be consummate, decorated with happy lanterns

but, now, it feels like I were living in the last house in the world

where the night wipes my shadow from the balcony

and the play of the crickets adds to the hollow in a corner of the wall

I know that one quiet day after another

---

[3] Translator's Note—this is Rilke's remark that goes: "I am too alone in the world, and yet not alone enough", see the link here: https://www.goodreads.com/quotes/235176-i-am-too-alone-in-the-world-and-yet-not

will bud, ear, flower and come to fruition, and it will have a summation

but in another country

—always, of course, and must

www.ingramcontent.com/pod-product-compliance
Lightning Source LLC
Chambersburg PA
CBHW021138090426

42740CB00008B/837